Save Now or Die Trying

Save Now or Die Trying

ACHIEVING LONG-TERM WEALTH IN YOUR 20s AND 30s

Mark Bruno

John Wiley & Sons, Inc.

Published by John Wiley & Sons, Inc., Hoboken, New Jersey.
Published simultaneously in Canada.

Wiley Bicentennial Logo: Richard J. Pacifico

For general information on our other products and services or for technical support, please contact our Customer Care Department within the United States at (800) 762-2974, outside the United States at (317) 572-3993 or fax (31 7) 572-4002.

Wiley also publishes its books in a variety of electronic formats. Some content that appears in print may not be available in electronic formats. For more information about Wiley products, visit our Web site at www.wiley.com.

Library of Congress Cataloging-in-Publication Data

Bruno, Mark.
  Save now or die trying: achieving long-term wealth in your 20s and 30s / Mark Bruno.
      p.   cm.
  Includes bibliographical references and index.
  ISBN 978-0-470-12141-2 (cloth)
  1. Saving and investment. 2. Savings accounts. I. Title.
  HC79.S3B78 2007
  332.024'01—dc22
                                                      2007009238

Printed in the United States of America.
10 9 8 7 6 5 4 3 2 1

Contents

Preface: Confessions of the Author

I have crunched a lot of numbers. And I have crunched a lot of numbers on top of these numbers.

I've read the research, pontificated with the pundits, and extracted everything I could from the experts.

And then along the way I forgot.

I focused on building an argument and then presenting some basic, yet fundamental solutions to the problem.

I became so completely committed to doing this every day that I just lost sight.

This is real.

This is not some warning on the 6 o'clock news that you may or may not go blind from eating too much Taco Bell.

This is about the way we live.

This is about the way we want to live.

And, ultimately, the way we think about how we want to live.

I talked to a lot of really good people who volunteered to let me peek into their lives and their thoughts. We focused on now and we talked about later.

But I forgot.

This is not about now, and it is not just about later.

This is about Always.

Money doesn't buy happiness, but being strapped won't help your chances.

One day, if I am lucky, I will be old. I'm not just talking about your early or mid-60s when you're newly retired and mostly concerned with finding some new hobbies to keep busy. At that point, it's your choice to stop working so long as you are ready.

But I'm talking about being 80, when I may not be able to work if I want to. I want to be around. I want to keep seeing the world and I want to keep learning. I want as much time with my wife as possible. And I don't just want grandkids, I want great grandkids.

I have always wanted things to be on my own terms and I don't see how that's going to change at all as I get older.

I'm 29 right now. More than 50 years from being 80.

No matter how far away that may seem, no matter how many numbers I may crunch, and no matter how many reports I may read, I shouldn't lose sight.

I shouldn't forget.

This is real.

Always,

MARK

Acknowledgments

I could not have accomplished even a fraction of this work without the personal and professional help of dozens of people who devoted their time, knowledge and support to this book. First and foremost, I thank my wife Wendy who has tolerated and endured my thoughts and tangents for longer than I can remember or comprehend. I also thank my family—Mom, Dad, Craig, and Helen—who have encouraged my behavior and absurdities since birth. Thank you, too, for not just nodding. To my editors and publishers at Crain's, particularly Nancy Webman, Chris Battaglia, and Bill Bisson. I thank them because they enabled this idea to become a reality—and for listening and supporting this endeavor as well. To my editors and eyes at the Wiley family—David Pugh, Michael Lisk, and Stacey Small—thank you for giving these words life and attention. Thank you as well to Cynthia Manson for finding this book a home and for your resolute spirit and enthusiasm for this project.

I also thank the countless professionals who allowed me to pick their brains and who shared their expertise, time, and thoughts. A significant portion of this book includes excerpts from interviews with these experts who devoted their careers to studying retirement, money management, and personal finance. They include David London, CFA, Elara Capital; the National Association of Personal Financial Advisors; Dallas Salisbury and the Employee Benefits Research Institute in Washington D.C.; Melody Hobson, Ariel Capital Management; Matt Schott, TowerGroup; Craig Brimhall, Ameriprise; the Center for Retirement Research at Boston College; Mark Warshawsky, Watson Wyatt; the Cato Institute; Kevin Bannon, Bank of New York; Cary Carbonaro, Family Financial Research; Rick Meigs, 401kHelpCenter.com LLC; Ellen Breslow, Smith Barney; Lori Lucas, Callan Associates; Bruce Primeau, Wade Financial Group; David Wray, Profit Sharing/401(k) Council of America; Morningstar; Yannis Koumantaros, Spectrum Pension Consultants;

the Employee Benefits Security Administration; Eddie Kramer, Abacus Planning Group; Georgia Bruggeman, Median Financial Advisors; Scott Cole, Cole Financial Planning; Marvin Rotenberg, Bank of America; Jeff Zures, Sanchez & Zures LLC; Pamela Hess, Hewitt Associates; Deanna Garen, Prudential Retirement; William Gale, Brookings Institution; Dr. Peng Chen, Ibbotson Associates; Steven Schwartz, Wealth Design Services; Ted Benna, 401(k) Association; Steve Utkus, Vanguard Center for Retirement Research; Pension Research Council; Don Salama, New York Life Investment Management; Cheryl Hancock, Rinehart & Associates; Sid Blum, GreenLight Advisors; Diane Pearson, Legend Financial Advisors; Morgan Stone, Stone Asset Management; Timothy Maurer, The Financial Consulate; Linda Leitz, Pinnacle Financial Concepts; and James Kibler, president of Eldridge Financial Planning.

Save Now or
Die Trying

No One Will Reward You for a Job Well Done

There is a pretty good chance that you could die broke.

And there is even a pretty good chance that you could go broke long before you die.

There, I said it. Someone had to break it to you.

I'm no alarmist—far from it—I just know the facts. It's not easy to consider your retirement when you may have just started working, or even if you've barely hit the halfway point of your working life.

But no one is looking out for us, no matter what you've been led to believe about retirement.

No one will pick up the tab when you stop working.

No company. No government agency. No parent.

It is up to You to assume responsibility for You.

In theory, our parents and our grandparents had a simple formula for retirement: work at the same company for a number of years and accumulate a pension that would pay you a guaranteed and defined benefit for the rest of your life. You keep working, we'll manage a huge fund for you while you work, and then we will cut you a check when you retire. And not just a paltry couple of hundred bucks each month. How does the average salary for your last three years of work sound?

Sounds great.

How about we pay you that amount until you die?

Just show me where to sign.

For many, a pension agreement like this was a reward for being loyal. It was a competitive tool for recruiting new employees.

It was a standard, simple, and defined benefit that people could depend on to take care of the bill for life after work—not to mention that every month a check from Social Security would also show up in the mail to fill out the rest of their retirement income.

It was a promise that was the backbone for millions of people in their retirement. It was never a right—it was a privilege and, perhaps, the best benefit an employer could ever offer.

But you and I probably don't have that benefit. These types of traditional pensions are disappearing at a rapid rate. We likely won't have a guaranteed lifelong pension that our employers take care of while we pay them back with loyalty and hard work. Companies just can't afford it anymore. Either that or they just don't want to be saddled with a seemingly never-ending commitment.

But there is more to our retirement story.

During a time that fewer people are taking care of us, we are also taking care of more people.

We are living longer, the older population is growing rapidly, and the Baby Boomers are royally screwing us. They are going to take more than we can give. There are just too many retirees and we are not a large enough workforce to support them. More and more people are drawing on a limited pool of Social Security supported by us, the working population, while we are supposed to cross our fingers and hope that there is a little something left over for us in 30 or 40 years.

Even if the system is dripped dry, Social Security alone is still not enough to live a decent retired life on. The average Social Security check a retried person receives now is about $960 a month.[1] That's barely enough today—and what we get in 30 years and what it will buy us then is anybody's guess. There is even the possibility that Social Security, as we know it, may no longer exist by the time we are in our 50s and 60s.

Yet you and I will also probably live longer than previous generations. Our retirements may last for 20 to 30 years.

We will still have to battle inflation along the way, so even if we do save, we have no way of truly knowing if it will be enough to live comfortably.

Sound the alarm.

You and I will not be given anything.

We may have to work longer than our parents.

We may live longer than our parents.

Without some decent planning or a trust fund, there are only two simple solutions to our generation's potential retirement crisis:

- Work forever
- Die sooner

But we don't have to watch our golden years change to brass. We don't necessarily need to work into our 70s either. We just need to wake up. We need to plan a little earlier and plan a little more than our parents.

Most importantly, we need to recognize that we have some major advantages over previous generations:

- We have time.
- We have greater access to information.
- We have more options.

Companies can cut pensions and the Baby Boomers can suck up all of the Social Security, but the one thing that we have right now that no one can take away from us is *time*.

We just have to be aware—aware of the options that our employers give us, aware of just how important thinking about and planning for your retirement is right this second. We also need to be aware of the most considerable investment force of our youth: *the power of compounding*.

Albert Einstein was once quoted as saying, "The most powerful force in the universe is compound interest." So don't just take my word for it, Einstein was a pretty plugged-in guy.

"Compounding" doesn't sound that cool; but you need to know what it entitles you to if you start saving now, even if it definitely doesn't sound inviting or remotely interesting.

Compounding is simple. You make an investment. You make money off of an investment. Rather than spending what you have earned, you leave it alone and allow your initial investment, plus whatever you have just earned, to continue generating more investment income. Repeat.

It's the snowballing effect. Start with a small amount, and then just keep rolling. Consider the classic example: Would you rather have $100,000 cash right now or would you prefer to receive one penny today, and I will double what I give you every day, for the next 30 days? You can probably guess where this is going. Forget the $100,000. If you started with 1 penny and your pay was doubled every day, you would be earning $5.4 million after 30 days.

That's the power of compounding. As long as it keeps rolling, it will get larger and larger. It's a simple concept, but it could have an incredible effect on your life.

With your retirement savings, if you continue to contribute the same amount of money to the same investment every year, your potential to get a larger return will increase because you are continuously working off of a larger pool of capital (which is just another fancy way to say money).

Consider that if you put away $1,000 a year every year for the next 30 years, you won't just have $30,000 waiting in your account. You could accumulate almost $110,000 if your investments produce just average returns.

For us, this isn't about getting rich quick. It's just the opposite. The idea of getting rich slowly may not be that attractive, but it's secure. It gives us the freedom to take new jobs, to take stabs at entrepreneurial ventures, or maybe even retire a little earlier than our parents and grandparents.

If we learn to leave our money alone, or learn about the new ways to increase the amount of money we save, and if we learn how to take advantage of all of the different retirement options out there right now, we could be staring at retirements that are *even more stable* than previous generations.

It won't be easy, but it's also not that difficult either. You just have to do a little work to put yourself in a position to make it happen.

So would you rather have this proposition or the quasi-promise of an old school pension from people at your company who you have never met? People who don't have nearly as much of an interest in you as you . . .

Outside of understanding just how important it is to start thinking about your retirement right now, the power of compounding is the most critical thing you should take away from this book.

It's not just enough to understand how it works. It's only a powerful tool if you start to take advantage of it now. They younger you are when you start saving, the more you will have when you will need it most. Every day that you delay, you reduce your compounding power.

You can wait until you're 40 to start saving for retirement and you will end up with what seems like, on paper, a pretty decent haul when you approach the beginning of the end.

But the truth is it won't be nearly enough for you to retire for very long. If you wait until you are 40 to start saving for retirement, you will have to continue working longer than you expected, or you will have to find some form of work during your retirement years.

Or you will just have to play Mega Millions until you either hit the right numbers or die.

Because if you wait too long to save for your retirement, you will almost certainly outlive everything that you have put away in just a matter of years.

If, however, at the age of 30, you made the same commitment to start saving, you will be set for many more years after you retire.

But don't take my word for it; numbers never lie.

Say you're 40 years old, you make $50,000 a year, and you have no money saved for retirement right now. You want to retire at 65 and you can't live on less than $40,000 a year. If you put away 10 percent of your salary now until you turn 65, and you get pretty good returns on your investments (let's assume 9 percent), your retirement savings will run out at the age of 73 if you withdraw $40,000 each year after you have retired.

Eight solid years and then nothing.

Now look at the same scenario for a 30-year-old today with the same salary, same contribution to retirement, and same returns on investments. If the 30-year-old also retires at 65 and withdraws $40,000 a year for retirement, his savings will last him until he turns 84.

He put away 10 percent of his annual salary for 10 more years than his 40-year-old counterpart, and the 30-year-old can now *fully* support himself during retirement for *11 more years of his life.*

I told you that the numbers don't lie—your ability to turn small amounts of money into considerable amounts of wealth will never be greater. To get an idea exactly how much power you have at a young age, consider Figure 1.1. It illustrates how much $10,000 would be worth when you turn 65 if you put that money away when you are 25-, 30-, or 40-years old. (assuming 8 percent returns).

As you can see, there is no contest. When you turn 65, the value of $10,000 saved at the age of 25 will be more than *three times* the value of $10,000 saved at the age of 40. It's the same dollar amount saved, you are just allowing yourself 15 additional years to let the

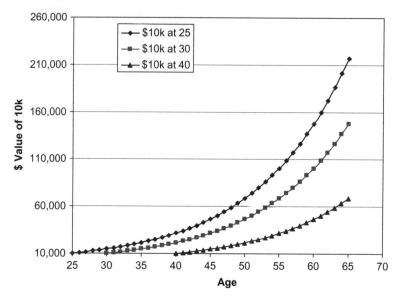

Figure 1.1   How much $10,000 would be worth when you turn 65

money go to work for you. And in the end, you will have $217,245 waiting for you, as opposed to $68,485.

As far as I can tell, there is only one downside here: It may not be as exciting as going to a casino with $10,000 in your pocket and turning it into $217,000 in one weekend. Saving your money is not instantly gratifying. It takes time and it is boring. But you need to know just how powerful you are right now—and how much you could be leaving on the table every year you wait.

You also need to be aware that no matter how much money you think you may inherit, or how much the house you don't own yet will be worth when you sell it in 30 years, you will not have nearly enough money to maintain your current lifestyle during retirement if you do not start saving now.

I talk to my friends and peers about retirement probably more than I should and definitely more than they want me to. Most, while they tend to acknowledge that their retirement is too far away to take seriously, have done some rough mental math about how much they may inherit from their parents and grandparents.

Many, if they haven't done any estimates of what their grandparents' condo in Florida will be worth one day, have at least considered that they're in somebody's will somewhere and should receive something at some point. That Money from Nowhere, I've been told, will probably help pay off mortgages or put kids through colleges, and maybe even help pay for parts of their own retirements.

They tell me that they have considered the future in some form, but just not in its entirety.

There may or may not be this Money from Nowhere as we move down the road. But there will certainly be an entirely new breed of Expenses from Everywhere that we can't even think about right now.

Besides paying for the basics such as food and shelter, you will also have to pay for your medical and health care expenses, which in and of itself could be enough to drip your savings dry. Just like many employers are cutting back on paying out lifelong pensions, fewer companies are offering health care and medical benefits to retirees.

While two out of every three large companies used to dish out health care benefits to retirees in 1998, that figure declined to one in three large companies by the end of 2005.[2]

And now for the kicker—for a person retiring right now, health-care and medical expenses will add up to a total of $90,000 for men and $110,000 for women over the course of their retirement, according to a study from Fidelity Investments last year.[3]

Add another $200,000 to the retirement bill for any retired couple.

You don't have to be a victim. Life doesn't have to be as unfair as it may seem. What you do with your money now, in your 20s and 30s, will make the difference in the quality of the life of your future self. You just have to buy into your future and never look back.

You probably have other things on your mind right now besides retirement, as you should. If you just started working, it's probably impossible for you to conceive that you will be working for another 40 years, let alone how important it is to think about retirement. But you are not on your own here. If I didn't back my way into job writing about retirement and other people's money, it probably wouldn't have occurred to me either.

People much smarter than me, with much more money than me, helped me to recognize that if I fail to commit just a small portion of my income to retirement right now, I am essentially forfeiting the ability to have more money when I will need it most.

Without putting money in the right place right now, you and I are passing on the chance to have hundreds of thousands of dollars—our dollars—waiting for us when we are set to stop working.

You don't need to be an actuary to understand the new math that's at work here. A penny saved in your 20s is 14 pennies earned when you hit 60, and you don't have to watch *Mad Money* every night to get those types of returns.

You need to know that your job is probably offering you something that is not as simple or as clearly defined as your father's or your grandfather's pension plan, but that's okay. Many jobs give you the option to enroll in a retirement plan that could take a little time and effort to get going and maintain, but it could prove to have an even greater upside than a traditional pension if you start using it early enough. And it might even help you purchase your first home or put your kid through school if you need it. You just need to know what you can do with your retirement plans once you start saving.

You need to know that no matter how little you may be earning right now, you can still find money to put away for your retirement without cutting back on your Starbucks consumption. Not everything in life has to be an either-or proposition. You have the money. You just may not realize it yet.

You also need to know that no matter how *much* money you may be making right now, you should probably be putting away more for your retirement—not to mention that you could be making better decisions with your investments.

You need to know that, even though it requires you to take money out of every paycheck, you will actually have a good shot at increasing your take-home pay if you contribute. You use pretax dollars to contribute to a 401(k), for example, which means you lower your taxable income by saving for your retirement. In new math, that would be:

Larger contributions = Lower taxes

You need to understand the long-term power of your early retirement contributions, and the investment income your money will earn over 30 to 40 years.

You need to know that more and more companies are willing to match the money you donate to your future. You also need to know that more and more companies are going to be automatically enrolling you in 401(k) plans. But first you might need to know what a 401(k) plan is.

––––––––––––

As if you needed more incentive to save for your retirement, many of your employers are giving you money to save.[4] Think of it as *free money* because that is exactly what it is. You need to know just how foolish you are if you don't take as much of their money as possible. Your job is paying you to save. You wouldn't turn down more money if they offered it to you up front. You'd take the money because it is why you get out of bed and go to work every single day. Instead of a signing bonus, consider it a leaving bonus.

"The truth is, with all of these options, people in their 20s and 30s are actually in a position to have greater security in their retirements than previous generations," says Dallas Salisbury, president and CEO of the Employee Benefits Research Institute in Washington D.C. "They can have it all."

You also need to know that there is no such thing as the Point of No Return. It is never too late to start learning and asking questions.

We are the information generation, a Google search away from every answer to every question we could ever ask.

It just has to occur to us to ask, even if it may seem like only the most basic of questions.

"So many people, when they get to a certain age, are embarrassed to ask simple questions about money and finance," says Mellody Hobson, president of Ariel Capital Management in Chicago, and a regular contributor for ABC's Good Morning America. "And they end up never asking and never learning the most basic things about money management because they are afraid of looking ignorant."

But you may be more than just a novice when it comes to finance. Even if you can describe the difference between a mutual fund and an exchange-traded-fund, there is probably a lot you don't know about some basic savings techniques that can net you huge gains over the course of the next thirty years.

Maybe you think you're okay because you have a 401(k) plan, but no IRA. Maybe you're like me and you've had four jobs in six years, which means you may also have multiple stagnant accounts that never vested.

Maybe you don't even know what "vested" means.

Maybe your new job won't let you participate in a retirement plan unless you spend at least a year at the company. Maybe you're at a job that doesn't even offer you any retirement benefits. There is plenty that you can do in the interim to create your own individual retirement account and start laying the foundation for your future financial security—because you don't have a choice.

No matter how little or how much you may earn during your working years, you can't afford to wait because you are not entitled to a retirement.

Fair or unfair, the burden of preparing for life after work ultimately falls on the individual, not your employer or the government. In other words: You.

That version of your grandfather's guaranteed pension—the defined benefit plan—is not a dinosaur yet but it is in the fast lane to extinction. Just consider the numbers: In 1980, there were 30.1 million American workers in the private sector who were covered by these pension plans, according to the Department of Labor's Employee Benefits Security Administration.[5]

At the end of 2002, that number dropped more than 25 percent to 21.6 million. And it isn't that people are getting kicked out of these pension plans—some companies have terminated their pension plans altogether, while others are just closing their pensions to new workers. That's me and you.

It is important to note, however, that while millions of private sector employees have been covered by defined benefit plans, there were also millions more who were not. Without the promise of a pension for many, there was the belief that Social Security payments alone would be enough to see major portions of previous generations through their retirement.

Those who currently rely on Social Security alone are now living on less than $1,000 per month.

We should not be caught as unprepared.

We at least know that we are probably not going to be getting a guaranteed pension anytime soon. And we know that we will need more than just Social Security to maintain a reasonable version of our lifestyles when we retire.

In a way, this is perhaps the most distinct advantage we have over previous generations. We now *know* the burden of our retirements rests squarely on our shoulders. Because we can be free of illusions, we can, and should, know to start planning earlier.

It's not just about blindly saving pennies in a jar the day you start working. We have some newer, more sophisticated options in retirement savings that could provide us with a more stable retirement income than any other generation.

During the same period that these old school pensions became less prevalent, there was a substantial increase in the use of defined contribution plans. These are retirement plans like the 401(k) in which you are in control. If your employer is a public school or religious organization, your defined contribution plan may be a 403(b), while state and government employees will often have 457 plans. These types of defined contribution plans will all be referred to as 401(k)s throughout this book, otherwise it will seem like you are getting beaten over the head with a series of barcodes or gym locker combinations.

With these retirement plans, *you* now define how much or how little to contribute to your future—the old model merely fixed how much you got paid out during your retirement. With defined contribution plans, this is now entirely up to you. Your payout will be largely based on how much you put in. The more you contribute, save, and earn, the more you will be able to withdraw for your retirement.

Plans such as the 401(k) also allow you to decide how your money is invested. Previously, workers had no say in this part of the savings process. This can be a great advantage, if done properly. And lucky for you, some new developments in the investment management industry, coupled with some new legislation from the federal government, have made it easier on you to invest your retirement money more effectively and—this is the best part—without even really having to do much at all.

There is a pretty good chance that you have access to a 401(k) plan, even if you aren't aware of it right now. Almost 53 million private sector workers were covered by these defined contribution plans at the end of 2002, up roughly 270 percent from 14.4 million at the end of 2002.[6]

And the gap continues to widen between old school pensions and defined contribution plans, perhaps more dramatically in the last few years than ever. Pensions were almost never regular subjects covered in business sections of daily newspapers or magazines. Now it seems like you can't go a week without reading that some major company, or even state-run government entities, are closing their old pension plans to new workers and pointing us in a new direction. They're steering us to the 401(k) plan instead.

———————

There will be employers, banks, brokers, books, websites, and friends to help you along the way as you save and invest towards your retirement. Part of the difficulty is that most of the information on retirement that is available is not geared towards people our age. You've seen the commercials: an older couple on a beach walking with their dog, the husband throwing a stick off into the horizon.

They don't have a worry in the world. They have more money than you and I do. And they will get more assistance than you and I will. Financial institutions want to help *them* because they have a deeper wallet, which means more of their wallet can be had. The more money you have, the more money banks, brokerages and fund companies can profit from you.

Most of the information out there right now is targeting these people—people who are closer to the end of working rather than the beginning. The economics just make more sense for those seeking profits.

This just means that you will often have to seek out the answers when you have questions. Again, nothing will be handed to you. Never be afraid to ask what you think is a dumb question. When it comes to your money and your future well-being, there are no dumb questions, only dumb decisions.

The questions you ask and the decisions you make in your 20s and 30s determine whether or not you will have to play catch-up for the rest of your life and, ultimately if you will live the life that you deserve to live once you stop working.

If you can stop working.

CHAPTER 2

Plan Now, or Die Broke

Americans seem to live and breathe and function by paradox; but in nothing are we so paradoxical as in our passionate beliefs in our own myths.
—John Steinbeck, *America and Americans, Paradox and Dream*

I was not born to be an expert in personal finance. I was, however, born to rationalize my spending.

It is a skill, as misguided as it may be, that I share with millions of other people who have become known to many as Generation Debt, a term we owe to the title of a book by *Village Voice* columnist Anya Kamenetz. It is a brilliant book and I suggest you read it when you get done with this one.

I live for the promise of a future payday, without really knowing when that may be or how long it could take for me to get there.

I live for now and I am banking on a very uncertain certainty. Sounds reasonable enough, no?

It's not that it is easy to spend more than you make, it's just more enjoyable.

When I finally nailed down a job in Manhattan writing for a magazine, the first thing I did was find an apartment in the city that basically cost me more than half of my take-home pay each month.

I rationalized that if I lived and worked in the city, then I could work more. If I could work more, then I'm more likely to get promoted and make more money to pay off my debt. Hey, it's not like

I'm going to grad school. I won't need it with all of the real-world experience. And, if I was in grad school, I'd have accumulated $50,000 worth of debt in a few years anyway. So clearly I am ahead of the game by only being $4,000 in the hole.

Sounds reasonable enough, no?

If I brought lunch to work, then I could afford to go out later that night. If I skipped dinner, then it would take fewer drinks to forget just how much actual cash I was spending on nothing.

New math, once again:

Short-term gratification + Disregard any future consequences
= Whatever outcome you would like

Beautiful.

I convinced myself that money-related issues will always find a way to resolve themselves over time.

False.

It wasn't until I started writing about retirement that I realized a few things. One, writing doesn't pay that well. So the debt will just keep getting larger if something doesn't change soon. Two, when I spent money on nothing, I wasn't just waving good-bye to my short-term cash; I was losing the long-term potential to accumulate that future payday that I have banked on since I started working.

We can cover our credit card debt, but we can never recover the power we have in our early working years to turn a fraction of our money into thousands of dollars of retirement income.

It's not about being money savvy. It's just about changing your perspective and making a commitment.

I'd rather be disciplined than smart any day.

Your paycheck already has line items subtracting medical and dental insurance, Social Security, federal taxes, and state taxes—all "life expenses" that you may or may not actually understand or use. And how many bills do you pay every month for cell phones and cable television that also have line items for mysterious expenses?

FCC charges on my cable bill?

Periodic finance charge on my credit card?

My cell phone bill alone has 11 line items under "Taxes, Fees and Surcharges" that total roughly $10 a month, including 911 services and "State Telecom Excise" charges. I have no idea what any of these things mean, but I can't get rid of them. I suppose it's the small price

I pay—$120 a year—for the privilege of paying T-Mobile for basic cell phone service every month.

These are all meaningless expenses that don't entitle us to anything of material use or understanding—yet, without agreeing to pay them, we can't receive the services we want. We know we can't fight it, so we mentally disregard it and just sign the check every month.

So why not commit to making retirement just another "life expense"?

Retirement is another line item in our lives, one that nobody is requiring or forcing us to pay. Except this expense is an investment in our future well-being.

Consider it a payment to your future self. Not only do you get to keep the money you commit to your retirement, the earlier you begin saving, the more you will have when you need to live off of your nest egg.

A Different Way of Thinking

Most people I know rationalize their spending as a defense mechanism. It makes them feel better, rather than worse, when opting for indulgence over prudence.

But what if we used our rationalizing abilities in a different way? Instead of opting for defensive rationalization—starting with a conclusion and then putting things in the proper perspective to support the desired outcome—I could probably use my skills to rationalize proactively.

In other words, before it's too late.

For instance, Matt Schott, a senior analyst with consulting firm TowerGroup, introduced the concept of "prepurchasing" retirement in a report published in early 2006.

He believes every dollar we save now could be viewed as *buying* a piece of our retirement, almost like a time share of sorts. While compounding can certainly be a powerful tool, it's not necessarily the most compelling argument for saving because there is no tangible or accessible *immediate* reward.

According to Schott, if you save a dollar today, rather than spending it, you have elected to put away a definite and quantifiable portion of your income for your actual retirement. The younger you are, the larger the amount of your retirement that you can "prepurchase."

Looking at savings in such a way might help to convince more people in their 20s and 30s that putting away small amounts of money, even though it might not seem like much when you consider may need more than $1 million to retire, translates into a literal and significant step towards accumulating enough wealth for an adequate retirement.

In his report, Schott uses the example of a 25-year-old who is saving $100 each month for his retirement. If you figure that the 25-year-old is earning 7 percent interest on the money he saves, then he's looking at $1,284 at the end of his first year of saving.

"Even if he understands the power of compounding, the accumulation of assets seems too slow to eventually reach his goal," he notes in the report.

But what if the 25-year-old didn't look at his savings in terms of gradual gains? What if, Schott says, he looked at it as a portion of his future retirement? By putting away $100 per month for a year, compounded annually, the 25-year-old has just prepurchased 18 percent of the income he will need in his first year of retirement.

Saving 4 percent of your income now directly purchases 18 percent of your income later. Not a bad deal.

And say this individual chose to double his savings to $200 per month the following year. With just two years of putting away $3,600. Schott estimates that the 25-year-old has then prepurchased the majority of the income (72 percent) that he will need in his first year of retirement. Add Social Security payments to the mix and almost an entire year's worth of retirement income is accounted for and secured.

Such a rationale "gives the 25-year-old a more vivid sense of the value of saving $100."

With saving for your retirement, you can't do it all at once. No matter how daunting the idea of saving hundreds of thousands of dollars may seem, it *can* be done with small dollar amounts over time. In addition to understanding the power of compounding, it's equally as critical to have the proper perspective on the value and future buying power of a dollar. "In many cases, life is a trade-off," says Schott. "You can have the leather seats in your car now, or you can choose to buy a part of your retirement instead."

Again, it's not about getting rich quickly. There aren't a lot of legitimate opportunities in life to succeed on that front. It's about saving early and building wealth gradually and slowly.

"There are four basic ways in life to become wealthy," says Craig Brimhall, vice president of retirement wealth strategies at Ameriprise

Financial. "You can inherit money, you can marry it, you can steal it, or you can accumulate it."

To get decent returns on your money, you don't need to play the market or know the exact differences between growth and value investing, for instance. You just need to have a basic understanding of what kinds of investment options your employers and financial services companies are offering.

Also, and perhaps most importantly, you should realize that you don't have to sacrifice too much of your take-home pay to make a significant contribution to your future. You *will not* cripple your current lifestyle by setting aside money for your retirement right now. In some cases, by putting money towards your retirement, you will actually end up actually increasing your take-home pay every year, but we'll get into that more specifically in Chapter 5.

You need to know that if you work for a company that has a 401(k) and offers to match all or at least part of what you contribute to your retirement, that should be the first thing you do to start your retirement savings.

But you also need to know that you can set up your own retirement accounts—either in addition to your employer's plans or independent of any other sponsored retirement plans—that can help you accumulate additional years of income for when you stop working. Individual Retirement Accounts (IRAs), no matter what your age, should be part of your foundation for retirement planning.

You need to know that when you turn 25, if you start contributing $4,000 a year to a Roth IRA, you could have a personal retirement account worth $1.1 million waiting for you when you turn 65 (based on a compounded average annual return of 8 percent). And with the Roth IRA, the IRS doesn't come after you for a penny if you wait until retirement age to tap into your money. You're using after-tax dollars to fund this account and, unlike other IRAs, you can't deduct your contributions from your taxes each year. But because you're paying when you plant the seeds for your retirement with a Roth, you are free from paying taxes when you harvest your crop later in life.

While many financial planners consider the Roth a no-brainer for young people, you will have other tax-advantaged options to build long-term wealth.

Other retirement accounts, such as the traditional IRA can help you amass a nice amount of money as well. That same investment of

$4,000 a year beginning at 25 years old would still help you accrue the same $1.1 million by the time you retire. The difference here, however, is that the IRS can tax the earnings and hit you for almost $300,000 (assume a 15 percent tax rate) over the course of time that you withdraw from your IRA during retirement. But, with the traditional IRA, you can deduct your contributions from your income taxes each year. This will get you a decent little short-term break, but it will have a huge impact on you over the long-term. While you may be able to write off the investments now and get a larger rebate on your taxes every year, you will get slapped with hefty income taxes when you take the money out for your retirement.

We'll discuss this in further detail in Chapter 7, but just knowing that one simple nugget of information about retirement accounts right now could help you have an additional $300,000 for when you will likely need it most.

So again, it's not about being all that savvy, it's really just about being aware and committed. And no matter how much I can rationalize my spending versus saving needs right now, it's hard to ignore the value proposition of saving for your retirement *at this very moment.*

Take the Roth IRA example again. The Roth IRA proposition is telling you this: put away $160,000 of your money over the course of 40 years and I, the Roth IRA, will produce an account that is worth an additional $1 million by the time you are ready to start your retirement.

I repeat: a Roth IRA could make you a millionaire if you agree to save your own money over time.

You might not think that you can afford to put away money for a retirement, which is really just a distant concept to many of us right now. But with that kind of money on the table, can you really afford to wait?

––––––––––

There will always be life issues to balance with your savings, whether it's paying off credit card debt, buying a house, or sending children to college. But your retirement is arguably, at all times, your most important life issue.

You can always take out loans to put a kid through school. You can take out a mortgage for a house. But you can't take out a loan to cover for your retirement.

It's not that you may not be aware of retirement; you may think about it here and there. Your own parents might be retired, or close to retirement, so it's clearly present in many of our lives in some capacity. It's just that many of us aren't doing anything about our own retirements right now.

In a survey of almost 700 young workers ages 18 to 30, two-thirds of those polled said that retirement is definitely on their radar. I suppose any majority should be encouraging, so good for us, no?

The problem, however, is that only half of the young workers surveyed reported that they are not saving for retirement at all. And more than half said that their biggest fear about retirement is not having enough money to live comfortably in the future.[1]

So let me get this straight: For most of us, it's on our radar *and* we fear that we may not have enough money to support ourselves when we are retired. Yet most of us don't do anything about it anyway?

I may be born to rationalize, but I am having a tough time coming up with any sort of defense on this one.

No matter how you perceive retirement, or whether or not you are saving for it right now, you are not alone. And you are not on your own either.

Throughout this book, you will read about some real people and their real lives—nothing like the "real" 20-somethings you see on MTV's *The Real World*. These aren't people who were handed P. Diddy-like digs or a dream job running some sort of Outward Bound program in Colorado.

These are people you probably know—the people you work with, grew up with, or went to college with. Some have already made it, others have not, and most are still stuck in the middle.

Most don't want to talk about their lack of planning or saving. Denial is a powerful coping tool. When I scoured and asked for peers to profile in this book, most people thought they had nothing of value to add. I asked a college friend, now a 32-year-old engaged male in New York City, to tell his story and his e-mail response probably sums up a lot of the informal feedback I received:

A. I have no money.
B. My retirement plans are very "loose" at the moment.
C. I don't do anything for free

D. At the very least, I will need some guitar tracks on some new songs I am recording in exchange for my time.

E. There just had to be an E.

Truth is, he is not broke, but like many young adults he just doesn't think he has money to spare for anything other than short-term expenses.

He is lying to himself, and we can prove it. Real financial advisors have offered their commentary and suggestions on how each of the people profiled should be investing for their retirement based on their specific life scenarios—scenarios that are probably a lot like yours in more ways than one.

Yet while this book offers a number of guidelines and suggestions, the most important thing that you should take away is this once again: No one will take care of *your* retirement except *you*.

It doesn't take care of itself. You can play catch-up, but you will die trying to recoup the savings power you had in your 20s and 30s. Retirement is a long-term investment. The longer you wait to plan and save, the more money you lose.

And the more you know now, the more you will have later.

3

The Truth, the Whole Truth, and Nothing But the Truth, So Help Me God

THE FACTS BY THE NUMBERS

We Are at Risk

Don't just take my word for it. If there wasn't a decent reason for concern, a lot of incredibly smart people at the Center for Retirement Research at Boston College would not have had to launch the "National Retirement Risk Index" last year.

Overall, there is a pretty good chance that most Americans will not be able to live the same lifestyles during their retirement years as they did while they were working. The index showed that if households work up until the age of 65 and tried to live off of all of their current financial assets, 44 percent will be "at risk of being unable to maintain their standard of living during retirement."[1]

And guess who is most likely to be at risk here? Anyone who is young, has a low income, or lacks pension coverage.

You, you, and you.

And if you're three out of three, don't jump. Please. You have time.

Most of us are at least one out of the three, and many of us are probably two out of three because of the general lack of pension coverage for younger workers.

The problem is that we are not increasing our financial assets at the same rate we are losing potential sources of retirement income such as traditional pensions and possibly Social Security.

It is a scary proposition, especially when you consider what it might cost for us to be retired in 30 or 40 years. Our costs of living will increase over time, that's a guarantee—but we may also live well into our 80s or even our 90s. Are you prepared to support yourself for 30 years after you retire? If you don't know, ask yourself this: Do you want to take a chance and find out when it may be too late?

Didn't think so.

How Much Will We Need to Retire?

If you are 30 or 40 years away from retiring, it's next to impossible to figure out exactly how much money you will need to support yourself for a prolonged period of retirement.

For now, figuring out "the number" shouldn't even be a concern for most of us. You have to walk before you can run, and for now, we need to concentrate on just putting one foot in front of the other.

Many financial advisors are now telling people who are about to retire that, as a rule of thumb, they should have at least 10 to 15 times their current annual salary socked away before they can even consider retirement. You may ultimately need 20 times your income to be safe, but let's just work with the lower end for now. (To lead a reasonable lifestyle once you stop working, advisors also generally say that you will need to draw about 70 percent of your final working salary during retirement.)

If you have never had a concept for how much retirement costs, figure that if you are currently earning $60,000 a year and you are approaching your retirement soon, you will need to have saved $600,000 to $900,000 to support yourself comfortably.

While that figure alone should leave your jaw hanging, that's just roughly what it would cost to retire in the immediate future.

But we may be 20, 30, or 40 years away from retirement, and we must consider that inflation will exponentially force our costs of living to be significantly greater.

If salaries and inflation were to both increase at the same rate for the next 30 years—figure an increase of 3 percent for both—someone earning $60,000 now would be making an annual salary of $145,000 per year in 2037.

Using this income as a point of reference for our future costs of living, that would place a minimum price tag of nearly $1.5 million on our retirement in 30 years.

We will grow up to be a generation of middle-class millionaires.

If we are lucky.

A False Sense of Security

But wait, there is always more.

The Baby Boomers are not helping us. It's not their fault, but there are just too many of them and they are living longer than ever.

Those of us who will be working for the next 30 or 40 years, as fair or unfair as it may seem, will be supporting the Baby Boomers in their retirement much more than they had to support their previous generations.

As more people retire from the Baby Boom generation—those born in between 1946 through 1965—the government will have to dish out more money in Social Security payments to support them. Social Security payments are still a vital source of income for many retirees, with the average retired person collecting a check for almost $1,000 each month.

These payments to retirees come from you, the worker.

That's just the way Social Security works—it is a "pay-as-you-go" system. The Social Security taxes taken out of our paychecks are not saved, nor are they invested, for *our* retirements. You Social Security payments don't go into an individual account that's waiting for you at retirement.

Our taxes go to help pay the benefits of people who are currently retired.

In this current Social Security system, a younger generation is always working and paying taxes to support an older generation. When we retire, we have to hope that the working population is large enough for us to draw a decent check each month from the Social Security system.

This wouldn't be such a major problem for us if it wasn't for one thing: When the Baby Boomers start retiring in 2010, the retired population will increase much faster than the working population.[2]

At the end of 2005, according to the Social Security Administration, there were roughly 3.3 workers for every retiree receiving Social Security benefits.

To put that in some perspective, turn back the clocks a few decades. Go back to 1940, when the ratio of workers to retirees on Social Security was 42 to 1.

Just two decades later, in 1960, that ratio dipped to five workers for every recipient.

Now factor in the retirement of the Baby Boomers. When this entire generation is retired by the year 2030, the Social Security Administration estimates that there will be roughly 2.2 workers for each retiree receiving benefit payments.

"The numbers should speak for themselves," says Mark Warshawsky, director of retirement research at Watson Wyatt, and the former assistant director for economic policy at the U.S. Treasury Department. "For the past few decades, people have been very lucky. These numbers should tell younger people that it's not prudent to think that they will be as lucky as previous generations."

Also, it's important to note that people—including us—are now living longer than ever. So, not only will we be supporting more people, but we will have to support them for a longer period of time. And we will also need more to support ourselves for an extended retirement period as well.

The population of the United States nearly doubled to 294 million from 1950 to 2004, according to the Center of Disease Control and Prevention, with the average American life expectancy increasing to 77.6 years old from 68.2 during the same period.[3]

More significant, perhaps, is the growth of the portion of the population ages 65 and older. This group grew twice as rapidly as the rest of the population. There were 36 million Americans over the age of 65 in 2004, compared with 12 million in 1950.

At the same time, the number of people over the age of 75 increased at an even more significant clip—there were 18 million people ages 75 and up at the end of 2004, versus 4 million in 1950.

Spinning these number forward, the CDC has projected that the population growth from now until 2050 will slow down a bit, but the population of older Americans will continue to grow more than twice as fast as the total U.S. population. Consider Figure 3.1.

Over the next 10 years, people between the ages of 55 to 64—the oldest of the Baby Boomers—will be the fastest growing segment of the adult population. At the same time, many will also begin to enter their retirement years and will start drawing on Social Security at record rates.

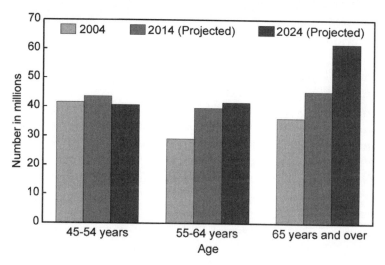

SOURCE: Centers for Disease Control and Prevention, National Center for Health Statistics, *Health, United States, 2005*, figure 30.

Figure 3.1   Aging of the Population 45 Years and Over

Over time, even after the last of the Baby Boomers hit 65 in 2029, the older portion of the population is expected to continue growing at an incredible pace, further reducing the ratio of retirees to workers to almost two workers for every retiree.

And finally, by the time the last of our generation turns 65 and hits retirement age in 2050, we will make up roughly 21 percent of the total U.S. population—almost twice the size of the current 65+ population.

So what does all of this mean to you? There are two major factors in play here.

For one, there is the near-term effect. If more people are counting on fewer people to pay for their Social Security, you and I will likely end up paying higher Social Security taxes in the interim as a result. At the end of the day, this cuts into our ability to find money to save for our own retirements.

Today, we pay a Social Security payroll tax of around 12 percent of our gross salaries, double what the rate was in 1960. The Social Security payroll tax is already the biggest tax that most households most pay, and it will probably be increased soon to pay for the upcoming group of retirees' benefits.

The Cato Institute, a Washington D.C.-based think-tank, estimates that the payroll tax will have to be raised to more than 18 percent to support the retirement of the Baby Boom Generation.[4]

The second factor of the Social Security dilemma that will impact our generation is more long-term. It may affect us when it becomes time for us to collect our retirement checks.

Michael Tanner, director of health and welfare studies at the Cato Institute, believes that because there will be fewer workers supporting more retirees, the growing Baby Boomer population will gradually drain the available Social Security funds that have accumulated over the years.

This means that you and I will likely receive a reduced rate of Social Security payments when we retire based on the way the current system is structured.

By 2017, the amount of Social Security benefits paid out to retirees is estimated to exceed the amount of money that the government collects from workers.

By 2040, without any major reforms to the system, the country's Social Security funds will be totally exhausted, and Mr. Tanner says that the government will only be able to payout retirees using the money it will concurrently be collecting from payroll taxes.

As a result, in the year 2041, retirees will receive reduced Social Security payments that are roughly 25 percent lower than expected. I am 29 years old right now, which means that in the year 2041 (sounds like a Conan O'Brien skit) I'll be turning 64 years old. Just around the time I will probably want to retire. And that's when we're going to run out of money? I guess timing *is* everything.

The longevity issue doesn't have to be that complicated. Just know one thing: You will live longer than previous generations. The longer you live, the more you will need to support yourself and maybe even others in your life as well.

There is now a 40 percent chance that you will live to be 90 years-old. For married couples, there is a 63 percent chance that at least one person will live past 90.

Also consider another, perhaps less obvious, or less expected, impact that longevity will have on your financial situation. While you are trying to save enough to support yourself for what may be an extended retirement period, you may also need to lend support to your own parents if they outlive their own retirement reserves. About one in every five workers over the age of 45 is financially supporting at least one of their parents right now.[5]

So the good news is we are living longer.

But the bad news is we are living longer.

Somehow, 90 has now become the new 75. This just makes it even more important for us to maximize the accumulation potential that we have in our working and earning years. And not just our prime earning years, but *all* of our earning years.

Forget the idea of retiring at 65 and dying 10 to 12 years later. You may need to build enough wealth to support you for 20 to 30 years of not working. Social Security may or may not be there to help.

If it does wind up being there for me in 35 years, great. But if it's not? I don't want to find out.

We need to take advantage of everything people are willing to do to help us save. For some reason, we are still waiting . . .

Too Many Still Missing Out

While more companies are offering defined contribution plans such as 401(k) plans, which reward employees for opting *in*to their retirement, there are far too few young people who are currently participating in these types of sponsored plans.

The younger we are, the less likely we also are to put any of our money towards our employer's retirement plans. Only 18 percent of people between the ages of 21 to 24 take advantage of the retirement plans being offered to them through their employers according to a November 2006 report from the Employee Benefits Research Institute.

The numbers improve as employees age; but the increase is still not enough. Only 38 percent of employees ages 25 to 34 who are eligible for a sponsored plan actually contribute to their retirement.

These numbers spell out a pretty harsh reality. The vast majority of employed people under the age of 35 are shunning what will likely turn out to be their most valuable lifeline in retirement.

At a time when we may be able to afford it most—before we may marry, buy houses, have children, or pay for their education—we are squandering our best opportunity to accumulate wealth. Not only are we forfeiting an excellent time to build the foundation of our nest eggs, we are also leaving money on the table by denying ourselves the chance to collect matching contributions from our employers who are offering to put their money towards our retirement.

Why aren't we contributing? Most of us say that we can't afford it. More than 70 percent of us say that we do not save for our retirement when we are young because it gets in the way of our "day-to-day needs" according to a February 2006 survey of Generation X and Generation Y workers by benefits consulting firm Hewitt Associates.

Right behind day-to-day needs, we don't put money into 401(k)s because we need it more for "lifestyle purchases." A Louis Vuitton handbag. A 51-inch plasma television. A PlayStation 2, followed by PlayStation 3, and soon enough by the inevitable PlayStation 4 to replace its inevitably worthless predecessors. Disposable accessories and impulse buys are winning out over keeping and maintaining what we earn.

You and I probably know more people who have iPods than IRAs.

Our obsession with spending rather than saving is both a psychological and cultural phenomenon that is heading in a troubling direction. "It's almost as if we cannot accept sacrifice anymore," says Kevin Bannon, chief investment officer at the Bank of New York. "There is a failure to make tough choices. Instead of compromising, we borrow."

In 2005, for the first time since the Great Depression, Americans registered a negative personal savings rate for the year.[6] As a country, we saved minus 0.5 percent of our after-tax income. In 2006, we continued to maintain this negative savings rate *yet again*. Almost 80 years had passed without this rate falling into the red—and now it happens in consecutive years.

This obviously is not the Great Depression and you don't need to be an economist to realize that things generally seem to be pretty stable; our inability to save has occurred during a time in which employment growth has been strong, and income levels and housing values are both as high as ever.[7]

Add this all up quickly. It means that we are now dipping into our savings to fund our current lifestyles right before a period in which an enormous chunk of the population—almost 80 million people—will enter retirement. "It's a slow motion train wreck," says Bannon. "And it's a real crisis, no matter how you want to look at it."

CHAPTER

4

The Self-Proclaimed Freak

Maya is the most rational-thinking 28-year-old you will ever meet.

Maya is the most irrational-thinking 28-year-old you will ever meet.

Maya has over $17,000 in credit card debt.

But Maya has more than $25,000 already saved for her retirement.

"I know what you're thinking," she says confidently, but with a touch of humility. "I'm a freak. Believe me, I know."

She is also one of the most tuned-in young people you will ever meet. Sharp beyond her years, governed by a healthy ambition, and most importantly, she always knows how to find a way to feel like she is in control of her own life.

She remembers, on her first day of work when she was 21, sitting in an orientation session with other new employees. Hours of discussion on health and medical benefits, proper workplace behavior, guidelines defining sick days and vacations. It didn't stop. Just a hazy blur of policies and programs only interrupted by coffee and bathroom breaks.

She let her mind wander. While most of her friends headed to New York for work, she opted for a job just outside of Washington D.C. She knew she wasn't going to make a lot of money at first, and she knew what little she made would go further just a few hours down I-95.

She was now wondering not *if* she would ever make more money, but when.

But then they showed her the bar graph. This PowerPoint presentation was different from all the other mind-numbing orientation materials.

It had dollar signs and lots of them.

There was something about the last few bars on the right side of the graph. They towered over the others, especially the last one.

She had heard somebody say something about retirement, but she wasn't paying all that much attention to the words. She was mostly intrigued by the huge numbers, the peak, at the end of the bar graph. They showed her how much money her 401(k) would be worth when she turns 65 if she started making relatively small contributions to her retirement immediately.

New slide.

The excitement is gone.

This graph was less intriguing.

The dollar amounts on the last few bars were not nearly as inviting. There were hundreds of thousands of dollars missing from the previous slide of pleasant dreams.

"It was this frightening-looking chart," says the former journalism and communications major, who claims never to have had an affinity for finance or math. "I could barely understand it, but I didn't need to. It scared the hell out of me."

At that moment, Maya was at least 40 years away from retiring, but it still hit her. She considered her father, reckless with his own money, approaching his own retirement with only a little more than nothing. "I know how I want to live," she says. "And I don't want to live like that."

Fast forward seven years and three jobs.

Maya has not used her credit card once in the last four years after racking up about $9,000 in credit card debt in her first three years out of college. Since then, she's added almost $8,000 to her debt from only making just the bare minimum payments to her credit card companies, which allowed finance charges and interest rates to take over her statements every month.

But somehow, incredibly, she never decided to stop contributing to her 401(k), no matter that her debt kept getting bigger every month.

And unlike her credit card payments, her contributions to her 401(k) were well above the minimum. She always put in more than her company would match, putting up to 6 percent of her salary in her 401(k) when the company would only match up to 3 percent.

At some point, they stopped matching contributions, she says. So she just put in a little more money every month to try and make up for the difference.

She didn't just put her money in randomly though. She wanted to make sure it was invested wisely. She asked a friend, a financial advisor, to help her choose from all the different mutual funds offered in her 401(k). She confessed to him about her debt.

He was shocked.

She was embarrassed.

"I have a lot of years ahead of me in my career," she says. "At some point, I'll get a signing bonus or a commission check that will probably let me wipe out my entire debt in one shot."

If she skips out on saving for her retirement, she says she would never go back and make up for the lost savings. It's never occurred to her to take a loan from her 401(k) to pay off her debt. She calls her retirement money "sneaky savings" and considers it money she never had.

Even though she still hasn't made up for spending all that money she never had in the first place.

But she knows what she wants. She wants to marry her current boyfriend. She wants to take two vacations a year with her eventual husband and their eventual kids. She wants the security of wealth more than she wants to give off the impression that she has accumulated wealth.

She wants to be happy.

Forever.

She knows that nobody will give her the money she needs when she wants to stop working. And even though she likes working, she knows she wants to stop working one day. When she does, she wants to live the life she wants to live.

After all, Maya, like she says, knows what she wants.

Maya says she is willing to make some sacrifices now so long as she doesn't have to make major sacrifices later. Although, she will admit, that on occasion she has to have "that" pair of shoes even if it might cost $300 or $400.

But now her income is a little different from her entry-level years. Maya's more than tripled her entry-level salary of $24,000 in her seven years of work. A few months into a new job right now and she knows she will soon be pulling in a six-figure annual salary.

Now she pays cash for her Manolo Blahnik's because she can. Now she uses cash for everything, even her boyfriend's car payments and his share of the bills while he tries to get his restaurant off the ground. She even waits tables for him a couple of nights a week to bring in some extra cash.

She is supporting herself and her boyfriend, and she knows that someday she may also be supporting her father, too. Yet she's still committed to supporting her future self. She is still contributing 9 percent of her salary to her new 401(k), even if her debt continues to mount.

She confesses that her credit card debt makes her nauseous. She's not kidding either. She pauses for a breath. "In the scheme of things, it's not that much debt. I'll be able to get rid of it easily at some point," she says, even if she doesn't really believe it.

Only a rational person could know what an irrational thing that was to say.

Prescription

First things first, Maya deserves credit for making a commitment to her retirement at such an early age. Even though she may have lived beyond her means in her early 20s, she can erase her debt and still wind up with a healthy retirement savings before she turns 30 and starts dealing with a new set of life expenses.

The first thing that Maya should do right now, financial planners say, is outline a budget and figure out exactly where her money is going every month. Putting together a budget is really the only way that Maya, or anyone for that matter, will ever actually know what she can afford to spend versus save. (If you have never done a budget, check Appendix B, Two Steps to a Budget to get a real look at your money picture and figure out how much you should spend and how much you should save each month.)

Doing a budget is the first step in getting serious about paying down her debt, which Maya needs to do as soon as possible, says Cary Carbonaro, a certified financial planner at Family Financial Research in Lake County, Florida.

"She is paying for past sins with that old debt," says Carbonaro, adding that Maya is at a point in her life now where she should start focusing her future needs, such as purchasing her first home.

According to Carbonaro, Maya can do two things to quickly erase her debt. First, she should take out a loan from her 401(k) and pay off a major portion of her credit card balance. (We'll get into the specifics of borrowing money from your 401(k) in Chapter 5.)

Because you're allowed to borrow up to 50 percent of your balance in your 401(k), Maya should borrow $12,500 from her retirement savings.

Furthermore, Maya will have five years to pay this loan back to herself. She'll have to agree to an interest rate on the loan, which will likely be close to 6 percent, but this rate is probably at least half or three times less than the rate Maya is already paying in credit card interest.

While she'll be lowering her interest rates, she'll also be paying the interest back to herself, not her credit card company. With a loan from your 401(k), you are borrowing your own money, so *you* are entitled to the interest, which will help to replace any investment income you might have earned on your 401(k) money if it had stayed put in your account.

Carbonaro recommends that as soon as Maya gets the check for $12,500 from her 401(k) administrator, she should immediately put it towards her credit card debt. She should have $241.66 automatically deducted from her a paycheck each month to pay back the loan to her 401(k). And perhaps most importantly, she should continue to contribute to her 401(k)—enough to get the full match from her employer—while she is paying back her loan. This way Maya doesn't leave any money on the table and she's also not significantly depleting her compound power.

This will leave Maya with roughly $4,500 in debt to pay off, which is a much more manageable amount. When putting together her budget, Maya should shoot to find an extra $100 every week that she can devote to paying off her debt for the next year. Even if it may mean some temporary lifestyle sacrifices, it will be well worth it over the long term. "She will have great freedom from the albatross of debt," says Carbonaro.

After one year Maya won't owe anyone anything anymore. She will owe herself some money that will take her another four years to pay back to her 401(k), but these loan payments are essentially just replenishing savings. She will be officially out of debt and able to prepare even more effectively for her future.

Even after Maya's final credit card debt is gone, she should continue to save $100 each week towards a down payment on a home. Maya is earning a good income so she should be able save this amount of money without much of a problem, especially if her boyfriend is able to contribute more to their expenses over the next year.

But Maya should also take her next pay raise and have it automatically deducted from her checks and put into an account to save for her down payment. She's already learned to live without that extra money, and she'll be taking one step closer to building equity (her home) that she can take with her for the rest of her life.

CHAPTER 5

Breathing Life into
Your Retirement

THE BASICS OF 401(K)s

Try googling 401(k)s and see what happens. You will come away with 165,000 search results, some links more informative than others.

Then go ahead and google the term "IRA." You want to know the difference between a Traditional IRA and a Roth IRA, and you get a bunch of info about the International Reading Association and the Irish Republican Army.

I don't care how little you may know about investing for your retirement, but you could probably deduce that neither set of hits is going to help you much with your finances or your retirement.

All of the information in the world is already at your fingertips, but it's almost impossible to know where you should even begin. Fortunately though, you have already succeeded in the first and most critical step of salting away money for your retirement—you are thinking about it and you are asking questions. You are becoming more aware that every day you wait to save for retirement, you may be potentially losing thousands of dollars.

You can't be expected to know everything there is to know about 401(k)s or IRAs. But you should have a basic understanding of what types of retirement investments are available for you and what is most appropriate for you and your lifestyle.

I wish that I could have taken a course in "Life Finance" when I was at the University of Maryland. But many of us can only learn as much as we seek out on the subject. I probably would have benefited more by taking classes on balancing a checkbook, as opposed to Entomology or 16th century British Literature. But basic money management, let alone retirement planning, just wasn't in the curriculum.

Yet, while no one will give you an official grade on your retirement planning and savings methods, it is a pass-fail class.

And you do not want to wait 30 years or more to find out if you will make the grade.

The two most important things that you need to know about and understand are 401(k) plans and IRAs if you don't want to fail Retirement 101.

Most young people I talk to have one or the other, but usually not both. A lot of people still don't even know if they are eligible or even participating in a 401(k), while most people can't tell me the difference between a Roth and a Traditional IRA.

And that's fine, you still have time and there is no better time than now to learn.

Both IRAs and 401(k)s are designed specifically to help you tuck away money for your retirement. While you should do everything you can to wait until you retire to tap these accounts, they can also be a pretty good way to hedge your savings for other life expenses that you will run into along the way to retirement. Just because you dedicate it to retirement now, the money isn't necessarily on lockdown until your 60s. If you need money for a home, for example, you could dip into your 401(k) or your IRA. You should set up other savings accounts for specific expenses, but having retirement accounts at least provides you with options and also makes sure that you are covering yourself for retirement as well. We'll dive further into the specifics in a bit, but it's important to know that saving in retirement accounts early in life will provide you with a lot of financial flexibility over the years. It never hurts to have choices.

By many accounts, the 401(k) is a best first option to start building your retirement savings. In large part, this is because you can pump a lot more money into a 401(k) in a given year than any kind of IRA. And you also may get more money from your employer for contributing to your 401(k), which will obviously help your cause more over the long run.

With the IRA, the advantage is that you have more investment options to choose from. You can basically invest your IRA money in any way you like, whereas in a 401(k) you have to choose from the investment menu you are given.

But to me, the difference in the amounts that you can contribute to a 401(k) ultimately outweighs the flexibility of an IRA. Here are the differences in the ceilings on contributions:

For 2007, anyone under 50 can contribute up to $4,000 to an IRA, and next year the limit will be raised to $5,000. With a 401(k), however, you can contribute more than three times that amount— the maximum contribution level for 2007 is $15,500 pretax dollars.

So let's start with the 401(k) plan.

First off, it's a terrible name for a wonderful thing. The term "401(k)" get its name from a section of the U.S. Internal Revenue Code that describes this kind of retirement plan. It was created in the late 1970s largely as an additional benefit for corporate executives; like the company jet, it was a benefit for only the most privileged individuals. (You wouldn't pass up access to the company jet, would you?)

The 401(k) is considered a "defined contribution" retirement plan that is specifically for private sectors workers. As mentioned before, if you work for a state or government agency, you will not have a 401(k), you will probably have a 457 plan. If you work for a public school, a church or another type of tax-exempt employer, your defined contribution plan is most likely a 403(b). They have their difference, but they are all essentially the same in their function for participants.

They are called defined contribution plans because you are the ones who decide how much, if any, money you will contribute to these plans. When you decide to retire, how much money you withdraw, and how often you withdraw funds, is largely up to you.

No matter how alien these retirement plans may sound, they are not complicated financial terms, so do not be intimidated. It is just a poor choice of "words" for something that has the potential to support you throughout the Golden Years of your life.

If we called 401(k)s the Get Rich Slow Plan or the Free Money Plan, I guarantee that participation rates would increase from the paltry levels that they're at now, not just for young people, but across the board.

Unfortunately, despite their tremendous upside, less than half of all working Americans under the age of 40 who are capable of being in a defined contribution plan actually participate, according to benefits consulting firm Hewitt Associates.

There are dozens of surveys from independent research institutes and benefits consulting firms just like this; but I have never seen a single piece of research showing that more than 50 percent of young people take advantage of the retirement plans they are offered through their employers.

"It's a sad, sad statistic," said Rick Meigs, president of 401kHelpCenter.com LLC, and coauthor of *Your 401(k) Survival Guide.* "Even if someone only put money into a retirement plan for just a few years during their 20s and stopped, they'd still have put themselves in a position to have potentially hundreds of thousands of dollars waiting for them at retirement."

While 401(k)s offer an incredible opportunity for both you and your employer to contribute to your retirement, there is one major hang-up: contributing to these retirement plans right now is largely voluntary.

Unlike the Social Security payments that are automatically subtracted from your paycheck, it has mostly been up to you, the employee, to decide if you will participate in a 401(k).

Help is on the way, however. New legislation passed last year, the Pension Protection Act of 2006[1], now encourages companies to automatically enroll its employees in 401(k)s. This type of adoption program is far from widespread right at the moment, although it is expected to increase significantly in the near future.

As of January 2007, about one-third of employers automatically enrolled their employees in a defined contribution plan, according to consulting firm Watson Wyatt. An additional 57 percent of employers polled by Watson Wyatt said that they are considering moving to automatic enrollment in the near future.

There is little doubt that over the next several years these new laws will have a major impact on participation rates. It is a serious attempt to change the shape and scope of our current retirement system, which requires us to *want and then choose* to participate in the system. If more companies, public employers and government entities move towards automatic enrollment, then people will have to choose to opt *out* of their retirement plans.

Right now, it's mostly an opt-in system, which clearly doesn't work for many young people.

Moving to an opt-out world is a good thing. No one will take away your ability to make decisions because you can always decline and drop out if you like. This is just the path of least resistance for employers; one in which you will still have the choice, but you will have to actively chose *not* to participate and save for your future. In employer-sponsored plans that automatically enroll new employees, on average, only about 10 percent of people actually opt out of retirement plans, according to Hewitt Associates.

If you are going to be automatically enrolled in a retirement plan, this makes it even more important for you to understand where your money is going and how it is being put to work for you.

This idea of automatic enrollment, in general, would put an employee in a retirement plan at default contribution rate, which means a small portion of your gross paycheck will be automatically deducted and funneled to a 401(k) before you get your actual net paycheck. It could be a low level, say 3 percent of gross pay, that is automatically subtracted. In addition, you have the option of increasing or decreasing your contribution, or opting out entirely.

In some cases, employers may even be gradually increasing your contribution levels for you until you ultimately receive the full match that your employer offers you. If they start you at a default 3 percent contribution rate, for instance, they may automatically increase your contribution by one percentage point of your pay for the next three years until you get up to 6 percent, if that is the maximum contribution level they will match.

And even though they are doing this on your behalf, you still need to know where your money is going and how it is being invested.

With automatic enrollment, your default contributions could go into relatively low-yielding default investment options. What does this mean? Instead of investing your retirement money in stocks, for example, which will give you the greatest chances to make money off of your investments over the long run, your money may be automatically placed in more conservative outlets, like a stable value fund or even a money market account. These types of investments are less risky than stocks, but they also have less upside. It means you could be forfeiting the opportunity to earn thousands of dollars.

Your employer wants you participating, but they probably don't want you to lose your shirt either. It's a compromise that is better than not participating at all, but it is still far too conservative to invest all of your retirement money in a stable-value fund at a young age.

In other words, you will be investing like a Grandma. You will still be saving money, but you just will not even come close to maximizing its potential.

As autoenrollment becomes more widespread, employers will try to improve these default investment options. They will hopefully move you into more personalized and targeted funds, or, at least, more efficient funds, that can invest your 401(k) money based on your age or risk tolerance.

Ultimately, your participation level is up to you—you need to be aware of what is being made available to you, and what types of short-term and long-term rewards you get in return for participating.

Are You Eligible?

If you have an employer, you are probably eligible to participate in a 401(k), or a similar work-sponsored retirement plan. If you are not sure, ask your boss, your human resources department, or your benefits administrator what types of retirement options are available to you as an employee of the company.

Odds are your employer offers you some kind of retirement plan even if you are not aware of it. Of the 154.7 million American who were employed in 2005, more than half—79.7 million people— worked for an employer or a union that sponsored a pension or retire ment plan.[2]

Some companies may make you wait awhile, perhaps a year or so, before you are eligible to join, but do not allow yourself to let that time come and go. If you have to wait, your employer will remind you when you become eligible to contribute. You don't have to do much here to get yourself up and running, but you do have to be moderately diligent.

If your employer does indeed offer a 401(k) plan, *this is the first thing you should be doing to save for retirement* and it should serve as the cornerstone for your nest egg.

"You have to start by using what is being made available to you," says Ellen Breslow, managing director of retirement and financial planning at Smith Barney in New York "The biggest mistake a young person could make is not taking advantage of the retirement offerings their employers provide."

A 401(k) is simply an account that allows you to invest a portion of your income, before it is taxed, specifically for the purpose of your retirement. As your money grows in a traditional 401(k), it will not be taxed; you only pay taxes when you take the money out for your retirement. This is what makes the 401(k) so extraordinary. With other types of traditional savings or investment accounts, you are putting away money that has already been taxed (your gross income) in accounts that will continue to be taxed on an ongoing basis.

Basically, outside of retirement savings, you put less to work and you pay more to do so.

With a 401(k), your employer essentially sponsors this retirement package on your behalf. It creates and designs a plan and presents you with a menu of various ways to invest your retirement money. In doing this, your company has gone out and done a lot of the leg work for you. It has reviewed a number of investment firms and selected investment products that will provide you with, in theory, the best opportunities to generate long-term returns on your money. This basic dirty work could take you hours, days, or weeks to do on your own. Or it could take you no time at all and you could end up making hasty and, perhaps poor investment choices. With a 401(k), your employer is your buffer.

The investment menu on 401(k)s will always vary, but in a basic plan, you are presented with an assortment of mutual funds that your employer has selected and will monitor on an ongoing basis. In a mutual fund, in its simplest form, qualified investment professionals invest a pool of money—your money plus all of the money of every other investor who has selected this fund—in a collective account that buys a certain style of stocks or bonds, for example.

The benefit of a mutual fund is that you have professional money managers running your money. You don't have to spend your days scrolling through Yahoo! Finance or buying and selling individual stocks that you may not really know anything about. But perhaps most importantly mutual funds offer you the benefit of diversification, which prevents you from being exposed to too much consolidated investment risk.

Look at it this way—if you invest in an individual stock, your money will take a direct hit if that stock performs poorly. If you buy a mutual fund instead, you could own this same stock, but it may be only one of about 20 or 30 companies in the overall fund. As a result, if this same stock takes a hit, the impact of that loss will be a lot less significant.

Here is an important side note for people who work at publicly traded companies that is discussed in Chapter 9, when we look at investing the money in your 401(k). You could be given the option to directly invest a part of your 401(k) money in your company's stock.

Be very careful here. Remember, diversity will be your friend over the next 30 to 40 years. Having too much of your 401(k) invested in your company—or any one stock for that matter—makes you incredibly vulnerable. Just ask anyone who worked at Enron and lost their retirement savings when the company tanked. As a rule of thumb, most financial planners suggest you have no more than 10 percent of your money invested in your company stock.

Your employer will give you a brochure that describes all of the funds that are available to you through your retirement plan. You will have to select the types of funds that you want to invest your 401(k) money in, which may not be that appealing to many people who are novice investors. You can, however, select only one single fund that will take care of all of your basic investment needs in one shot, and they will age with you until your retire. We get into that in Chapter 9 as well. You should know, however, that no one is asking you to be Warren Buffett here or a world market beater.

You will want to monitor your 401(k) over time. You won't want to do it so frequently that you are tempted to day trade when your funds are or are not doing well. You can get in and out of the funds in your 401(k) as often as you please. Nevertheless, remember, you are in this for the long-term. While diligence is critical, daily account management is not.

A 401(k) is ultimately an opportunity for you to take pretax dollars and put it in the hands of investment professionals—people who manage money for a living. They will plug your retirement money into the markets on your behalf in an attempt to gradually grow your account over the years.

Think of your 401(k) as a pyramid, with you on the very top. A portion of your income is at the pyramid's peak. It is then trickled down to your 401(k) sponsor, who helps disperse your money across several different types of investment vehicles. This money then goes down to another level of trained investment professionals who invest your money in a wide, diversified range of securities, which ultimately decide the investment income that you earn on top of the money you sock away for retirement.

You will also benefit now by saving for later. I promise.

Yes, you gain access to quality investment products and professional money managers through your 401(k). And by squirreling away money now, you may even be able to retire by the age of 60 and have a legitimate after-work income to support a decent lifestyle.

By contributing to your 401(k), you have acknowledged that it is important to take care of your future self, and you have accepted that no one is looking out for you but you.

You've grasped the single most important concept so far: the importance of participation.

But you deserve to get something out of it right now other than just a pat on the back.

There just isn't much fun in getting rich slow.

If you are anything like me, you want some instant gratification. You want more money, not less money, at hand for your normal costs of living and playing. Again, if you are anything like me, you want more money to help pay down any debts that you may have accumulated from student loans, or just from impulse purchases that felt like sound investments at the time. Yes—my $400 conga set sounded like a great buy seven years ago. Now it's in my grandmother's basement in Queens because I don't have room for it. And as cool as she is for an 89-year-old, my grandmother has no use for my congas either. I think.

That said, here's the best part of setting aside money for your retirement. If you contribute to a 401(k), you are actually putting yourself in a position to increase the amount of money that you can get from your employer over the longterm and in a given year.

Sounds crazy, but it's true. Numbers don't lie.

More and more companies are now willing to match every dollar that you put towards your retirement, up to a certain portion of your salary. The most common match is still 50 cents for every dollar that you contribute, and you will often get this match for up to 6 percent of your salary.[3] If you are getting a better match than that, then good for you. it is all the more reason to contribute.

If you are not getting a quality match, you might be getting an upgrade soon. As companies ditch their traditional pensions and steer new employees to 401(k)s, they are "enriching" their defined contribution plans to provide you with even more incentive to save. So maybe they only used to match 50 cents for every dollar you contributed. If they choose to enrich their 401(k) plan after freezing their traditional pension, you may be looking at a dollar-for-dollar match.

Or, in some cases, maybe the old amount that they would match would be up to 3 percent of your salary. Many companies are now enriching this to allow you to get up to 6 percent.

Not a bad haul for just deciding to opt in. Consider the dollars and the sense of it in real terms. If you earn $50,000 a year and your employer will match your contributions up to 6 percent of your pay (which is a typical match rate these days), your employer is guaranteeing you an extra $3,000 each year as a reward for saving for retirement.

So you put in 6 percent, which is $3,000, your employer will match it with another $3,000. No professional money manager, no matter how talented or resourceful he or she may be, can ever produce those types of returns year in and year out, let alone guarantee them. This employer match is essentially a no-doubt-about-it 100 percent return on your investment. All you had to do was opt in and then contribute enough to get that maximum match.

So you have just set aside $6,000 in your 401(k) in one year, and you only had to pony up half of that. Now you're in a position for your future self to make some real money: If that one year's worth of contributions earns a compounded investment return of 7 percent over the next 30 years, that $6,000 itself will be worth $45,674 upon withdrawal.

To drive it home one more time, you sacrifice 3 percent of your salary now and you can get back almost 100 percent of your salary later. And, if you are diligent enough to keep making these contributions for the next 30 years, your 401(k) would be worth $652,112.

And all you had to put in was $3,000 each year.

You don't have to contribute the $3,000 all at once either. You should have it automatically deducted out of every paycheck so that you don't have to think about it. We're talking about $125 from each paycheck for just one year, and when you retire, this annual contribution will be worth almost the same as your entire current annual salary.

As just a general saving rule, you should not be contributing to your retirement in a lump sum once a year. It is just too difficult to keep that money set aside—and personally I would have a tough time parting with it all at once if I wasn't immediately getting something back in return. When presented with the option to buy a 42-inch plasma television or save for my retirement, the TV just seems a little bit sexier. That's one of the beauties of the 401(k). It's an automatic payroll deduction, so it is money you can't spend. Trust me, you are better off this way. You can't lose what you never had.

What most people also don't realize is that your 401(k) contributions can give you something else back almost immediately. Here's the 401(k) cherry on top—remember, you are contributing pretax dollars to this account. That $3,000 you pumped into your 401(k) comes out of your gross pay. That's money that, if you "kept," a good chunk of it would have gone to the government when you pay taxes at the end of the year.

Most people I talk to who don't contribute to any kind of retirement plan say that they don't have the extra cash to do so. They say that if they contributed every month they would have to bail on gym memberships, dry cleaning, or, even worse, cable television.

The truth is, besides saving more of your own money, and in addition to getting more money from your employers who match your contributions, you are also lowering your overall taxable income.

Let's go back to the employee who is earning $50,000 again. She is contributing 6 percent of her annual pay to her 401(k), using pretax dollars. Her boyfriend, who is also earning $50,000 a year, is not using a 401(k). He's investing in a taxable account like a certificate of deposit or a standard money market account.

Guess who should be treating for dinner at least once a month? Take a look at Table 5.1.

Table 5.1 Contributing to Your 401(k) on a Pretax Basis Can Help You Increase Your Take Home Pay

	Pretax Savings in the Plan	Saving in a Taxable Account outside of the Plan
Annual gross salary	$50,000	$50,000
6 percent of pay before-tax contribution	−3,000	0
Taxable pay	47,000	50,000
Less a hypothetical 27 percent Federal income tax	−12,690	−13,500
6 percent regular annual savings in a taxable account outside the plan (from gross salary)	0	−3,000
Take home pay	$34,310	$33,500
Annual difference in take home pay	$810	

Source: Fidelity.

Forget that her investment in a 401(k) will produce greater returns over the longterm than a certificate of deposit (CD) or a money market account. Forget that she is also possibly getting another $3,000 from her employer as a match. She is earning the same salary as her boyfriend, yet she is taking home $810 more than he is.

If she's getting the full match from her employer, she's netting $3,810 more this year than her boyfriend. And again, they bring home the same gross salary.

So just when you think you don't have enough money to spare for your retirement, can you really afford not to save for your retirement? You are actually making less in some cases if you do *not* contribute to your retirement.

For me, that was the moment of epiphany.

The money in your 401(k) is growing tax-deferred, which means you will have to pay taxes on it when you withdraw. But, because you won't be paying taxes as your money grows along the way to your retirement, you will have a larger pool of money that can compound more quickly than a taxable account. You have a bigger snowball working for you. (With a brokerage account, for example, you pay taxes every year on the money you earn off of your investments.)

At the point of retirement, there is a good chance you will be in a lower tax bracket than you are during your working years. So even though you will pay taxes later on your 401(k) withdrawals, in all likelihood they will be lower during your retired years than they were during your working years.

Every Little Bit Counts

While I can't stress enough how important it is to contribute enough to get the maximum match from your employer, it's just a fact of life that not everyone will be able to comfortably contribute, say, 6 percent of their salary every year to a retirement plan. First things first, do a budget. Almost everyone knows what they earn, but not many younger people are aware what they spend. Don't guess that you can't afford to put money in and contribute. Figure it out. There is a worksheet in Appendix B that can help you crunch the numbers right now.

No matter how small the contribution at first, getting yourself in the right frame of mind early on about saving money should prove in the long run to be an even more powerful savings tool than compounding. "Every little bit counts," says Lori Lucas, senior vice president and head of the defined contribution practice at Callan Associates, a San Francisco-based investment consulting firm. "For younger people, getting a foot in the door can be the most important step."

If contributing enough to get the full match is truly out of your reach, most financial planners suggest that you at least get in the habit of dedicating some portion of your salary to a work-sponsored retirement plan. Even 1 percent to 3 percent of your pay is better than 0 percent.

This will allow you to get some momentum in building a decent retirement savings. It will also put you in a better position to increase your contributions in years to come. This is what Bruce Primeau recommends, the vice president of wealth management services at Wade Financial Group in Minneapolis.

If you are not contributing enough to get an employer match, Primeau suggests that you gradually increase you contributions over time, perhaps by one percentage point every year, or whenever you get a pay raise. "If you can't put in enough get to the full match right away, that's fine," he says. "But teach yourself to squirrel away at least a small portion of your pay at first; there will be opportunities for you to up your ante along the way."

Primeau and other financial planners agree that pay raises are an ideal opportunity for younger workers to increase their retirement contributions. You have already learned to live without the raise, so you won't feel the pain of putting some—or all—of the raise into an employer-sponsored plan, depending on how much the increase may be. Also, because you can contribute up to $15,500 to your 401(k) in a year, some advisors say you might want to consider putting all or part of your bonus in the account. Again, it's money you never had, so unless you *really* need it for other expenses (like paying off a credit card bill), consider your 401(k).

Waiting and Vesting

There is a chance that you might not be able to contribute to your work-sponsored plan—or get their matching contributions—right away. Your employers will sometimes want to be sure that you are going to work for them long enough before they open up their wallets and start springing for your retirement. Again, your employers aren't required to help you out with your savings. That's why they call a perk like a 401(k) a benefit in the first place.

Most companies will let you start contributing to a work-sponsored retirement plan as soon as you start working. As of November 2006, roughly 70 percent of employers allowed their employees to take advantage of their retirement plans immediately, according to a survey conducted by the Profits Sharing/401(k) Council of America. The remaining 30 percent of employers require their employees to wait no more than one year before they become eligible to participate.

Your employer will let you know when you are eligible to participate. They may send you an e-mail or a letter in the actual mail, but one way or another you will be reminded that you have the green light to go ahead and start using their plan.

If you are required to wait, *do not use this as an excuse* to avoid saving. Just because you are technically sitting in a waiting room does not mean you should completely forfeit one of the prime savings years of your lifetime.

Many financial planners suggest that if you are not immediately eligible for a 401(k), you should still save a portion of each paycheck as if you were contributing to your retirement plan. Don't wait until a few months have passed, start saving right away. Figure out what you would have contributed, and then have that money *automatically deducted* from your pay and sent to a savings account, or even a brokerage account, that will allow you to easily access the money. Treat it just like it is an actual contribution to your retirement. It will help you get used to living without a percentage of your paycheck— ideally enough that would have entitled you to the full match from your employer.

Remember, you can put up to $15,500 into your 401(k) in a single year right now. David Wray, president of the Profit Sharing/401(k) Council of America, suggests that when you do become eligible, you should take the amount that you have already saved and directly contribute it to your 401(k) provided that your total contributions for the year do not exceed $15,500.

If you're earning $50,000 this year and after one year your employer lets you into a plan that matches contributions up to 6 percent of your salary, start setting aside 6 percent of each paycheck now. You will have $3,000, plus whatever interest you earn during the year that you can pump into your 401(k) on your anniversary date.

After two years, your diligence will have translated into at least $9,000 in 401(k) savings: $6,000 of your own contributions and $3,000 in matching contributions from your employer. They'll only match up to 6%, or $3,000 in this case, no more.

Also, once you become eligible, your actual contributions will come straight from your *gross pay*, not the after-tax amount you take home. This will give you a little more breathing room on your paycheck once you're in the plan, almost like getting a mini-raise. You may even want to consider increasing the amount you save when you become eligible. You have already learned to live without more. So, if you can hack it, go for it.

While most employers will let you participate in their retirement plans right away, there is a decent chance that you won't be vested immediately. This just means that they will technically match your contributions right now. However, you are not entitled to keep their contributions unless you work for the company for a certain amount of time.

Even though they have given you the money on paper, if you chose to leave before you are fully vested, you can't take all of their money with you. *Their* money only becomes *your* property if you stick around long enough. "It's just a corporate philosophy that can serve as a pretty solid retention technique," says David Wray.

He also points out that roughly 40 percent of employers allow for immediate vesting, while about 12 percent of employers have "cliff vesting" policies that allow participants in a retirement plan to become fully vested after one or two years. With this set up, you will be 100 percent vested the day that you hit your target anniversary, but 0 percent vested during every day prior.

The remaining 48 percent of employers "graduate" their employees over three, four, five or six years, according to the Profit Sharing/401(k) Council. Under this kind of vesting schedule, unlike cliff vesting, you are entitled to partial vesting before you become fully vested.

With a six-year graduated schedule, for example, you might be 20 percent vested after two years, 40 percent after three years, 60 percent after four, 80 percent after five and 100 percent after six.

The free money is still there for the taking, vesting just requires that you make a predefined commitment to your employer in exchange for the maximum benefits that they are offering.

Employers realize just how often people change jobs these days, and vesting can be a good way to keep you from jumping ship too soon. After all, they want to get the most out of you just as much as you want to get the most out of them.

Life Happens

Even if things are going well and you are financially stable enough to contribute to your retirement without sweating, life does happen all the time. Being that we are still young, there will be more life decisions to make that will involve an entirely new set of expenses— buying a house, cars, having children, and paying for their college, for instance, are just a few of the things that you have to look forward to, if you haven't experienced any already.

Fortunately, with most 401(k)s, there are ways to access your money before you retire without having to pay any early withdrawal penalties, or without depleting the money you have worked diligently to accumulate.

The easiest and most common way to do this is through an actual loan that you can take out against your account, one in which you promise to pay the loan back to yourself over a set period of time.

By taking a loan from your 401(k), you are formally agreeing to borrow your own money from your account. You acknowledge that you must pay it back—with interest—based on a fixed rate that you work out with your employer or 401(k) administrator before you take the loan.

The good news here is that you pay the interest back to yourself because *you* are the lender, as opposed to a bank, who you would owe both interest and the amount borrowed. (This interest you pay to yourself, unlike with a typical mortgage, is not tax deductible, however).

The bad news is that some employers might stop matching contributions while you have a loan outstanding. Make sure to ask this question from your plan administrator when you are considering taking out a loan.

With a loan, you can typically take out up $50,000, or half of the total amount that has vested in your account. You also usually have about five years to pay it back, unless you are using it to buy a home, then you are often able to work out a longer-term loan.

Even if you are not of retirement age when you take the loan out, you won't be penalized for tapping into your account early. The only way you will be hit with an early withdrawal penalty is if you fail to pay the full loan back over the time period that you agreed to with your provider.

There is a pretty good chance that at some point in the future, when you're looking for a large chunk of cash to make a life purchase, your 401(k) will look like really attractive option. A first home purchase is a great example, given how many people buy their first apartment or first house between the ages of 20 and 39.

There are a number of pros and cons to consider before you make such a move; but as a rule, most experts say that you should not haphazardly borrow against your 401(k) to cover your credit card debts or pay for vacations, especially when you are young. Your 401(k) is not a piggybank. Rather, you should be looking at it as a last resort.

Typically, people do take out loans from their 401(k) to buy their first houses, and also to help pay for education.[4] You can take out a loan for almost any reason, but aside from these two instances, many experts strongly advise that you don't take out money from your 401(k) unless it's an emergency and you truly have no other options. Using the money to purchase or renovate a house, or to help fund an education, is essentially just another form of investment with some pretty strong upside. Both can help improve your financial standing and your future net worth if you play your cards right.

However, if you choose to take a loan from your 401(k), the most important thing to remember is that you *should not stop making contributions* while you pay off the money you borrowed, especially if your employer will continue to match any part of your contributions.

If you stop contributing to your plan while you are paying back a loan, it will make a huge difference in the amount of money you accumulate over the longterm. Consider the example of George illustrated by Morningstar to depict the differences.[5]

George

George, a 35-year-old participant earning $40,000 a year, wants a new car. He has $20,000 in his 401(k). He contributes 6 percent of his salary every year, which amounts to $2,400, and his employer matches with another 3 percent, kicking in another $1,200. In total he's putting in $3,600 a year.

If he keeps this up, George will have $583,723 waiting for him in his 401(k) at the age of 65 (assuming an 8 percent annual return on his investments).

But because he wants this car right now, he takes a $10,000 loan against his 401(k) and agrees to pay it back over the next five years at an interest rate of 5 percent.

If he stops making contributions during this period, his account will be worth $458,673 when he turns 65.

The decision to take out $10,000 and not contribute to his 401(k) while he pays the loan back will end up decreasing the value of George's 401(k) by $125,050 by the time he retires. His contributions during that time would have totaled only $12,000.

But let's say he still took out the loan and elected to keep pumping 6 percent of his pay in his 401(k). If George continued to contribute over that five-year period, enabling him to also get his employer's match, he would have $578,275 in his 401(k) at the age of 65.

In the end, it's still about $5,000 short of what he would have accumulated if he never took out the loan, but it's not nearly as bad as it could have been if he temporarily stopped contributing.

While taking out such a loan may seem like a good idea at times while we're young, remember that you may end up working longer as a result. You are potentially putting your power of compounding on hold—and ultimately draining a portion of your retirement income.

But the decision is yours to make, and nobody else's. You should know all of the facts, so here are some of the pros of taking out a loan from your 401(k).

The Pros

If you are buying your first home, for instance, and you have bad credit, then it may make more sense to tap into your 401(k), instead of going to a bank for a loan. One of the main advantages of taking out a loan from yourself is that you don't have to go through a credit check, making the loan process pain-free, not to mention more expeditious.

Also, you will likely get a better rate on a loan from your 401(k) than you will on a typical loan from a bank, especially if you don't have good credit.

You will work the rate out in advance with your plan, but it's often only slightly higher than the prime rate, which is a benchmark used by many banks to determine home equity lines of credit or credit card rates.

If you are ever looking to find out the prime rate, it's published by the *Wall Street Journal* every day. Or you could simply google "prime rate"—at the beginning of 2007, the prime rate was 8.25 percent.

It will always cost something for you to formally borrow money, even if you are agreeing to borrow your own money. At least with a loan from a 401(k), you are paying the interest to yourself and you are getting a rate that won't hurt your day-to-day finances as much. But as convenient and practical as it may sound, there are number of reasons *not* to borrow from your 401(k) as well.

Now for the Cons

There are "opportunity costs." For starters, you pay the loan back using after-tax dollars rather than with the pretax dollars that you used to fund the account in the first place. So you are re-funding your 401(k) with dollars from your take-home pay, not your gross annual salary.

When you pay back your loan, you are not paying it back dollar for dollar. If your loan payments add up to $360 a month with interest, for example, and you are in the 28 percent tax bracket, you will have to make $500 in gross earnings to cover that amount.

Translation: You will now be paying "double taxes" on 401(k) withdrawals in your life. You are putting in taxed money now to repay the loan, and then later in life you will be paying taxes again on the withdrawals you make for your retirement income.

There is also a second drawback. You are taking a calculated investment risk here whether you realize it or not. You have to hope that the total interest that you pay yourself back over the life of the loan will amount to more than whatever investment returns *you would have gotten* had you left the money parked in your 401(k).

If you are paying back your loan over the course of a weak market, this may turn out to be a really good play. If the markets are strong, you will end up forfeiting the chance to participate and pay a significant opportunity cost in the process.

Crossing your fingers is not going to help you here, either. Unfortunately, when it comes to timing the markets, you don't know until you know. This is why, if you choose to take out a loan from your 401(k), you should leave your stocks alone in your 401(k) portfolio and borrow from other parts of your 401(k) that have less potential to produce stellar performance such as money market or bond funds.

There are other real life risks that you are taking when you borrow from your 401(k). If you lose your job, or even if you decide to leave your job for another opportunity, you will have to pay the loan back well before it's due.

You may find that you have as little as 60 days, for instance, to pay the loan back in full. Otherwise, you will find yourself slapped with the 10 percent early withdrawal penalty and you will also have to pay income tax on the money as well.

Hardships Happen

Aside from a loan, the only other time you can take money out of your 401(k) is if you have a legitimate financial need, or what the IRS would technically consider a "hardship withdrawal."

This is usually for emergencies only and you will have to prove that you have exhausted every possible resource available to you other than you 401(k). Your plan administrator is responsible for sending you a description of all the documentation you will need to make your case.

Usually, you will qualify for a hardship withdrawal if you can prove that you need the money for one of six reasons:

1. To prevent eviction or foreclosure.
2. To cover unreimbursed medical expenses.
3. To make a down payment on your primary residence.
4. To make repairs to your primary residence.
5. For tuition payments for you or someone in your immediate family.
6. To cover funeral expenses.[6]

In any of these cases, you don't pay back the money you take out of your 401(k), and you can only take out exactly the amount that you can prove you need. You will also be hit with a 10 percent early withdrawal penalty and you still will have to pay taxes on the money that you take out. This is because it is not a loan and you will have to report it as income earned for that tax year.

If that's not enough of a price to pay, you also won't be allowed to contribute to your 401(k) for six months after you take the money out.

401(k)s Are Also Perfect for the Upwardly Mobile—Like You

With all due respect to my bosses, I just don't see myself working for the same company for the next 30 years. I wouldn't rule it out, but life doesn't work like that anymore. If it happens, then I'm fortunate. It means things had a way of working themselves out along the way before I decide to hang it up.

For the most part, however, I view myself as an independent contractor. I work for me. I lend my skills and talents to an employer in exchange for adequate compensation—and maybe the ability to learn from good and smart people who know a lot more than I do.

Realistically, I know that I get restless. I had four real jobs in my first six years removed from college. It drove my family crazy. My father had the same number of jobs in his 35 years of working. To many in the old working guard, I was a flake who didn't know what he wanted and couldn't commit to commitment.

But I'm no flake; I'm just slightly restless with a twist of independence. I, like many of you, am part of a new breed of American worker.

There is a good chance that you could have a dozen jobs before you hit your 40th birthday. In fact, the average American has now held 10.5 jobs between the ages 18 and 40 years old according to a career "longitudinal" survey released by the Bureau of Labor Statistic in August 2006.[7]

As we have become more portable, we have also needed retirement plans that are a bit more flexible than traditional pensions.

The 401(k), even though it has been around for almost three decades, is now essentially becoming the new primary breed of American retirement plans for the new breed of American workers.

These retirement plans, unlike your father's or your grandfather's pensions, are extremely portable. You can take your 401(k) with you when you leave. You don't need to collect eight different partial pensions from eight different employers when you retire and attempt to figure out how much or how little to expect from these companies.

Your 401(k) money is *your* money and you are free to do whatever you want with it over the course of your working life.

After you leave a company, you generally have four options for any savings that you may have accumulated in your 401(k):

1. You can leave your money where it is, you just can't contribute anymore and you obviously won't be getting any more money from your former employer. It just sits and accrues investment income over time.
2. You can take your 401(k) money to your new company, provided that it offers a 401(k) plan; you should review the plan and all of the investment options before you roll the money over just to make sure that you're satisfied with everything your new company has to offer. If you're not, you can . . .
3. Roll the money into an IRA. You can open a new IRA or you can roll it into an existing IRA's that you may already have set up. The key here, which is the same as with the first two options, is that you are allowing your money to continue to compound at its full capacity for years until you retire. The only way you give up the power of compounding is if you . . .
4. Liquidate your 401(k) and take the cash. You will have to pay hefty taxes on any of the money withdrawn, and you will also likely have to pay a 10 percent early withdrawal fee if you are not older than 59.5 at the time you take the cash. If you're young and still have a number of working years ahead of you, this is *not* a good option. And in the short-term, it hurts too. I learned the hard way and it cost me a few grand in savings and taxes.

The IRA is most likely going to be your best move when you switch jobs. With an IRA, you simply have more investment options. You can invest your money however you like, unlike a 401(k) where you are bound to the investment choices that are presented to you by your old or new employer. We look at the specific details of IRAs and rollovers in Chapter 7. For now, here's the most important thing you need to know about what do with your 401(k) money when you switch jobs: *Never take the money when you run.*

Unfortunately, this is a move that too many young workers still make. "There are so few Gen Xers who appreciate the idea of preserving their retirement capital," says Yannis Koumantaros, chief pension consultant at Spectrum Pension Consultants. He estimates that of the roughly one-third of Gen Xers that participate in retirement plans, two-thirds cash out when they take a new job. Add it up and this means that basically one out of every nine Gen Xers makes a move to rollover and preserve the money that they have already accumulated for their retirements.

No matter how much, or how little, you have built up in your 401(k), it never makes sense to cash out when you leave. Not only will you get hit with some pretty nasty penalties and taxes, you will also basically be starting over from scratch with your retirement savings. Your compounding power will take a serious hit, even if it's only a small chunk of money that you have taken out.

Usually when you withdraw your 401(k) money from your old 401(k) you have up to 60 days to make a decision whether to roll it over into your new 401(k) or an IRA. There is no need to let your decision linger. You already made the decision to commit to your retirement, so don't unwind all of your progress.

Even though it may seem like a small amount now, especially in the scheme of what you might need to retire, a little today can easily turn into a lot for tomorrow with proper patience and just the slightest but of planning.

What If I Work for a Small Company? Or What If I Work for Myself?

If your workplace has less than 100 employees, then you may be eligible for a retirement plan known as a SIMPLE IRA (Savings Incentive Match Plan for Employees). For your employer, these plans are cost effective and easy to set up, so many small businesses and nonprofits will opt for a SIMPLE IRA over a 401(k).

There are many similarities between a 401(k) and a SIMPLE IRA for employees. You make pretax contributions from your gross salary directly to your SIMPLE IRA and the money grows tax-deferred until you withdraw it for your retirement. You also choose how you want your SIMPLE IRA money invested, based on a menu of investment options your employer will provide you.

But unlike the 401(k), with a SIMPLE IRA your employer is required to match your contributions, or make what is called a "non-elective contribution."

If your employer chooses to match your contribution, they must match dollar-for-dollar, which is a great perk of the SIMPLE IRA. However, they are only able to match contributions totaling up to 3 percent of your annual compensation. So, while you get the guaranteed dollar-for-dollar match, that match caps out at 3 percent.

The other option your employer may go for is the nonelective contribution. This means that they will automatically contribute an amount that is equal to 2 percent of annual compensation for every eligible employee. If you choose to contribute your own money to the SIMPLE IRA, they'll put in 2 percent. If you decide not to contribute, they'll still put in 2 percent. With the nonelective contribution, you're guaranteed a contribution from your employer.

Another important difference between 401(k)s and SIMPLE IRAs are the contribution limits. With a 401(k), you could put up to $15,500 in your account in 2007. With a SIMPLE IRA, you can only contribute up to $10,050 for the year.

There are definitely some limitations here compared with the 401(k), but it can still be a powerful tool to help you accumulate retirement savings. It also helps that with a SIMPLE IRA, you don't have to wait at all to get going. Once you start contributing to a SIMPLE IRA, you are automatically 100 percent vested in the plan. So every contribution you make *and* receive from your employers is yours, no matter how long—or short—you stay with this employer.

For the Self-Employed

If you run your own business then you're not excluded from participating in a legitimate retirement plan—you will just have to start it yourself.

A few years ago, new tax laws went into effect to help out small businesses and their owners; in the process, the "Individual 401(k)" was born.[8]

These plans function just like a standard work-sponsored 401(k), except, of course for the matching benefits. But there are other advantages if you're eligible.

For starters, the Individual 401(k) is only an option if your business consists of just you and your spouse. If you have incorporated yourself, say as either and S-Corp or a C-Corp, then you should be able to set up one of these types of plans easily.

Most brokerages, mutual fund companies, or banks will help you set up one of these Individual 401(k)s, which can also be referred to as *Solo 401(k)s*. This is one of the advantages of having your own 401(k)—if you worked for someone else, you would have to choose from the fund options that your employer makes available to you in their plan. With an Individual 401(k), you can invest in any funds or investment strategies that the provider you're working with, such as a brokerage house, has to offer. While you're on your own with this plan, it can be much more flexible when it comes to how your money gets invested. Ultimately, the choice is yours.

This type of plan can also be more flexible when it comes to making contributions as well. The basic maximum contributions levels are the same as a standard 401(k)—you can put in up to $15,000 in a year as part of your salary deferral.

The contributions are tax-deductible. Your contributions and earnings both grow tax-deferred over the years, and are eventually taxed when you start withdrawing for retirement (remember, withdrawals are income when you are retired).

Another perk with an Individual 401(k) is that you can make a profit sharing contribution each year as well. This contribution can be up to 25 percent of your total compensation and is based on the income you report to the IRS. These contributions are also tax-deductible.

Combined, your two sets of compensations can add up to $44,000 in a given year, almost triple the maximum contribution anyone can make to a standard employer-sponsored 401(k).

With an Individual 401(k), you can also borrow money from your plan, something that you generally can't do with some of the older types of individual retirement plans like the SEP IRA. With an Individual 401(k), you can take out a loan under the same set of general rules as a standard 401(k)—50 percent of the total value of your 401(k) up to $50,000. You will have five years to pay yourself back the loan and the interest, unless you've borrowed the money to help purchase your primary residence, and in that case you can extend the duration of the loan.

Fees: Everything Has a Price

As with everything else in life, your 401(k) will have a cost, even if you're getting some money for free to participate.

Fees and fee structures can really vary widely from one plan to another, but there are some basic expenses that will usually be hitched on to most 401(k)s.

Unfortunately, you cannot always control all of the fees that you have to pay to participate in your plan. But you should know that your employer is obligated, by law, to make sure that the fees you pay are fair and in line with the normal costs of 401(k) services.

The first fee you will generally run into is an administration fee. Most employers don't actually run your 401(k) plans in-house. They farm the plan out to a service provider who specializes in overseeing retirement accounts.

Employers hire an administrator to take care of many of the day-to-day operations involved with running your plan. The administrator is essentially the hub for all of your 401(k) activities and questions—they handle the accounting, recordkeeping or legal components involved with your 401(k), and they may also be your point of contact for basic customer services questions, online access to your account, or even investment advice.

This all comes at a cost that your employer negotiates on your behalf. Sometimes your employer absorbs this cost. Sometimes you and I end up paying these administration fees, which can either be a fixed flat fee that comes right out of our account, or it could be a fee that is based on the amount of money in your account.

Your fees usually are disclosed on your account statements, your "summary plan description" (which you get when you join your plan), or your annual report that details all of the expenses and services involved with your 401(k). It may not be front-and-center, but it's in there.

There is not much you can do about this fee; it's just a cost of having a retirement plan. You should, however, always know what you are paying and where your money is going. The more services the administrator provides, the more you end up paying in administration fees. So, while you may not be able negotiate these fees down yourself, the best thing you can do is take full advantage of every service that is being made available to you—after all, you're paying for it. Any time you have a question about *anything*, call your administrator to get an answer. Whether it's a basic question about a loan, or you're looking for investment guidance—make sure you get the most out of what you are paying.

Investment management and transaction fees are the other expenses that you have to bear for participating in a retirement plan such as a 401(k).

Because you are given access to professional money managers, you have to pay fees for their services as well. Often when you buy or sell into or out of a fund, there is a transaction fee, or a sales charge, associated with your activity. Think of it as their commission.

Here there is not much you can do to work the costs down either, other than limiting your buying and selling. This is just another reason not to treat your 401(k) like a day-trading account.

Then there are investment management fees. This is an ongoing fee that you pay to a fund company for running your money.

It's often based on how much money someone is running for all of its investors and you usually see management fees described in terms of percentages, or "expense ratios." Basically, this percentage is how much it costs for a fund company to cover all of the overhead expenses associated with one fund.

You have a little bit of room here to lower these costs, depending on the types of funds that you choose to have your 401(k) money invested in. But you are still relatively limited because you can only choose from the funds your employer is making available to you.

The good news, however, is that the fees you pay for a fund through your 401(k) are generally lower than what you would pay if you directly invested in that same fund on your own. Because your employer, when they select a fund as an option in their 401(k) is basically buying in bulk, they are getting a wholesaler's discount on management fees. The reduced fees depend on your specific employer; but generally, the largest employers with the largest 401(k) plans tend to get the largest discounts. This is extended to you, which is yet another benefit of the 401(k). Not only are you contributing pretax dollars that grow tax-deferred, but you're also paying below market value for your professional money management services. You're getting an institutional discount.

Investment management fees can be all over the place; they will vary depending on the fund company providing the investment management and they'll also differ based on the types of funds you select.

Consider this basic rule with investment management fees—in theory, the more work a fund manager does for you, the more you pay for their services.

For instance, some funds offered in your 401(k) are "actively managed." This means that the portfolio managers who are running your money are constantly working to outperform the markets for their fund's investors. This involves continuous research as well as frequent monitoring and trading of all the different investments that the portfolio managers have made with their fund's assets. This doesn't necessarily guarantee that they will beat the markets, but it will cost you more because they are doing more work in an attempt to get you higher returns.

Other funds that you can choose are "passively managed." These funds do not attempt to beat the markets—instead they aim to duplicate the general performance of the market. To do this, a fund company mirrors a popular market index such as the Standard & Poor's 500 Index, which consists of the 500 "blue chip" stocks. These are generally large, well-established companies with strong earnings. As they go, so should the markets, in theory.

In duplicating the S&P 500, the manager buys the stock of every company tracked by the index. This involves much less research and less trading than with an active fund. It also may mean that you get lower investment returns, compared with an actively managed fund. As a result, you pay lower fees for a passively managed fund than one that it actively managed.

This can get tricky because paying higher fees does not guarantee that you always get superior investment returns. With active management, you're not paying for results, you're paying for the amount of work that someone is doing to attempt to get you superior results. You're paying for the chance to outperform.

At the same time, paying lower fees for passive investments doesn't necessarily mean that you won't get solid investment returns either. It just means that your investment returns will be consistent with the general market.

The passive versus active debate is one that we have run into a lot at *Pensions & Investments*. (As much as I would like to be writing about whom I think would win if the women from *Desperate Housewives* fought the women from *Sex & the City*, this is what we write about at P&I. But for the record, I'd put my money on the Housewives.) Both sides of the active/passive coin have merit; and the truth is there is room for both passive and active management in your portfolio.

It is important to consider fees—not just in your 401(k), but in all of your investment and banking transactions—throughout your entire life. Think of ATMs and taking out cash. If you aren't using your bank's machines, you are going to pay a $1 to $2 fee to access your money. And if you're only taking out, say, $60 in total, a $2 ATM charge is a 3.33 percent fee just to get at your own money. Think of that as a negative investment return. No more, no less.

When it comes to your investments, the fees you pay are essentially taking a bite out of any of the returns you are earning on your money.

Consider this example, which the Employee Benefits Security Administration points to in a recent report on 401(k) fees. Say you're 35 years away from retiring and you have $25,000 in your

401(k). If you assume that you will get an average investment return of 7 percent over the next 35 years, your current 401(k) account balance will be worth $266,914 when you retire—not including fees, however.

Over that 35-year period, if fees and expenses reduced your investment returns by 0.5 percent, your 401(k) value would be roughly $227,000 at retirement.

At the same time, if your fees reduced your investment returns by 1.5 percent, you would be left with a 401(k) worth about $163,000.

A 1 percent difference in fees paid over the course of 35 years would have reduced your balance by almost 28 percent.

Christine Benz, director or mutual fund analysis at Morningstar and coauthor of *Morningstar Guide to Mutual Funds.*, proposes that 401(k) participants should generally look for funds that have expense ratios between 0.50 percent and 1.5 percent of assets. Rarely, if ever, is there a case to use a fund that has an expense ratio of more than 1.5 percent. If you strictly chose the most inexpensive funds available in your 401(k), Benz says, "You could be doing far worse things with your investments."

According to Benz, most people tend to only consider two things about a fund: its past performance and its costs. "The investor who shops for the cheapest funds will usually be far better off than the investor who chases the funds that have had the best past performance," she says. "I'd rather see people look for inexpensive over hot any day."

If this sounds like a lot of work, or even just a lot to think about, you're not wrong, it is.

This is all part of the territory now. Participation is up to you. The responsibility, however, of looking out for your own best interests falls into your lap and to do so you should have a basic understanding of the sum of a 401(k)'s parts.

Fortunately, with retirement plans such as the 401(k) becoming the dominant savings vehicles for more people, things are starting to get a bit easier. There are easier ways now to pick the right funds, aggregate all of the expenses, and make sure you're on the right track as soon as you get out of the gate. You can get a lot of help now; as you will read in Chapter 9; or you can even elect to let someone else take care of your 401(k) for you entirely.

———————

One last point on 401(k) plans that is important to note, especially for those of you who are not sold on the reliability of these retirement accounts: It is difficult to ignore all of the stories of corporations filing for bankruptcy in recent years, particularly in three major industries: airlines, steel, and automobiles. These are, old school companies with old school pensions to match; a lot of these companies have ditched their pension plans because they're either too expensive to maintain or the impact on a company's balance sheet is just too unpredictable.

In many cases, when these companies have filed for bankruptcy, workers and retirees have seen their traditional pension benefits decrease significantly. When an employer files for bankruptcy, the assets in their traditional pension plans are not protected by law. They are backed by a quasi-governmental insurance agency, the Pension Benefit Guaranty Corp., an organization that can take over a bankrupt company's terminated pension plan and pay out a reduced benefit to retirees.

For many of these workers and retirees, they now receive just a fraction of the promise their employers made years ago when they were enrolled in traditional pensions.

The good news for anyone who participates in a 401(k), however, is that these assets are protected by federal law, specifically the Employee Retirement Income Security Act of 1974.

So even if your company goes belly-up, you're still entitled to your money. This law doesn't protect you from any investment losses; it just makes sure that your money continues to stay *your* money.

CHAPTER 6

Anything But Entry-Level

He might not know it, but Jake has a pretty good shot of growing up to be a millionaire.

Unless he gets scared.

He's not rich yet, but he's on the right path. He made $97,000 as a research analyst last year, his first year out of college, and he's got the apartment in Manhattan to prove it—not to mention the 61-inch HDTV.

He also has the bank account to show that while he spends, he's anything but reckless. After 12 months of working, he's managed to put almost $30,000 into a savings account. He did it with diligence, putting a couple of hundred dollars into his account from every paycheck. Every bonus and commission check he earned went straight into the bank, no questions asked.

He's debt-free, shares an apartment with his girlfriend, and he's making at least twice as much money as any of his friends. Money is definitely not an object and he appreciates how lucky he is.

But Jake isn't comfortable.

He's no fool. He knows that technically he's doing well. But while he won't come out and say it, he doesn't trust money.

"I've just seen how easy it can come and go," he says. "And it's scary."

Jake saw his father lose his job and he just can't seem to shake it, even though it took place almost 10 years ago.

But it wasn't just that his father lost his job.

His father worked for Enron.

He got laid off first, and then a few years later he lost almost everything when the energy company filed for bankruptcy in 2001, the same year that its stock plummeted from $90 a share to roughly 30 cents.

Like a lot of people who worked for Enron at the time, Jake's dad owned a lot of company stock—enough that he thought he could retire off of it one day and live comfortably ever after. This was supposed to be a sure thing. This was a *blue chip* company.

It wasn't supposed become worthless in the blink of an eye.

But it did. Jake's big house turned into a small house and his father keeps on working when he could have been retiring.

No wonder Jake doesn't trust money.

There is a reason Jake says that he put the $27,000 he saved into a standard savings account that earns about 1 percent interest. "I know I should be doing something else with it," he says. "It's not smart the smartest move, but it's my money. And I want it to stay that way."

He knows that he saves money like an old lady. He knows that his ultraconservative thinking is likely costing him in the long run. But he says he's not ready to risk parting with his money just yet. He'd rather tuck it under his mattress than pump it into a 401(k).

He says he has a 401(k) at work. He's just not interested in taking advantage of it. First and foremost, the company doesn't match any contributions. He believes there is no incentive to opt in.

He also says he doesn't like the funds that his company offers in its retirement plan; so even if he could look past the lack of any match, he can't find a good reason to use his 401(k).

He's heard all about IRAs. He knows how much money he could have when he retires if he just starts putting a little cash away right now.

He just won't pull the trigger.

It's not just fear that keeps him from doing anything with his money, he says. There are other things besides retirement that consume Jake.

An engagement ring.

Buying his first house.

Sending the kids he doesn't have to college.

"Life is ridiculously expensive," he says, as if he's never done the math before. "I don't know how people do it and then have any money left to retire."

Jake is saving for everything and nothing all at the same time.

He is confident, but not cocky, that he'll be earning a six-figure salary for the good part of his working life. The money will keep coming in, and whether it's fear or indifference that has him paralyzed now, he knows that neither is a good excuse to sit on his hands.

He knows he will have to do something with his money and he knows it should be for more than 1 percent.

He just doesn't know where to start. He doesn't know who to ask for guidance, and he definitely doesn't know who to trust.

Jake understands the costs of life and he also understands its risks.

But he doesn't really understand how much he is potentially leaving on the table by forfeiting his prime compounding years.

He doesn't understand that he could be a millionaire.

Soon.

If he isn't scared.

Prescription

Given his age, Jake clearly has a nice income and cash flow is fortunately not a problem. According to Eddie Kramer, a certified financial planner at Abacus Planning Group in Columbia, South Carolina, Jake nevertheless suffers from misguided beliefs about money.

To Kramer, Jake needs to have a better understanding of the risks involved with investing; and understanding risk is not the same as completely avoiding it. While Jake may have a basic understanding of the stock market and mutual funds, he needs to become more familiar with the concepts and principals of investing, rather than just the execution. For instance, if he had a better understanding of diversification, he might overcome his fears of losing money.

"His father may have lost all of his retirement savings because he was not diversified," says Kramer. "A large portion of his savings was invested in one company. He was invested in Enron in many ways. His wages and income stream were invested with Enron, and so was his retirement savings. There are a number of lessons that Jake should learn from his father's misfortune."

Enron may be perhaps the most extreme example of the risks involved with being too concentrated—if you have all of your money concentrating on one stock, or even one or two funds, you are more susceptible to risk. As that company or fund goes, so goes your money.

(Again, as a general rule, most financial planners and advisors suggest you never have more than 10 percent of your retirement savings dedicated to company stock.)

This makes it even more important for Jake to take advantage of his employer's 401(k), even though there is no match and he might not like the fund choices. For starters, he can begin instantly diversifying and saving for his retirement in a tax-efficient way through his 401(k). Jake can, according to Kramer, diversify how his retirement money is invested by either properly picking the right mix of funds that his employer has made available to him, or by choosing one fund that will give him instant exposure to several different assets classes, such as a lifecycle fund (see Chapter 9).

In addition to diversification, Kramer points out that Jake can also lower his taxable income by contributing to his 401(k), which allows him to increase his annual take-home pay. So, despite the lack of any match, it still makes sense for Jake to save in a 401(k), rather than a savings account that is funded with after-tax money where the gains are also taxed.

Kramer believes that right now Jake should consider dedicating 15 percent of his gross pay to saving for his retirement, with 11 percent of his gross pay going into his 401(k).

If he does this, consider the math at work in Table 6.1.

Not only is Jake putting himself in a position to let his money compound for roughly 40 years, but he's also increasing his take-home pay by almost $3,000 by contributing to a 401(k).

Table 6.1   Jake's Gross Pay and his 401(k)

Jake Could Either:	Taxable Investor Gross Income: $97,000 11% Contribution	Tax-deferred Investor Gross Income: $97,000 11% Contribution
Wages	$97,000	$97,000
Less: 401(k)	$0	($10,550)
Taxable income	$88,850	$78,300
Taxes	(19,209.50)	(16,255.50)
Taxable investment	($10,550)	$0
Take-home pay	$67,240.50	$70,194.50

If he puts 11 percent of his gross pay into his 401(k)—as Kramer recommends—then he should put another 4 percent into a Roth IRA, which would amount to roughly the maximum annual contribution level of $4,000.

Even though Jake earns a nice income, he would still be eligible to contribute to a Roth right now. (Anyone making over $99,000 is not eligible to make full contributions in 2007.) Given Jake's high income at an early age, it's possible that he won't be able to contribute to a Roth for much longer if his pay continues to increase. If Jake can only contribute for a few years to a Roth he will still have an account that can compound for 40 years or more and will ultimately be tax-free when he's ready to start taking out money for his retirement.

Outside of his retirement, Kramer recommends that Jake start considering his own timeline. Jake should seriously begin to think about when he might buy an engagement ring or when he will consider buying his first home. He also needs to think about his own job security, and he should establish an emergency fund immediately. Jake should have about six months of living expenses stashed away, or roughly $20,000, in a better savings account. Rather than settling for a 1 percent interest rate, there are a number of money market funds available that can offer an interest rate of at least 5 percent; Jake just needs to shop around a bit. "He's done a good job of saving for this, he's just been saving in the wrong place," says Kramer, who adds that in a money market account, Jake doesn't need to worry about losing his money either. It's federally insured and 100 percent guaranteed.

This would still leave Jake with another $7,000 in savings that he could put towards either an engagement ring or the money he'll need for a down payment on his first home. If either of these purchases are less than five years away, he should specifically earmark these life expenses and put them into a savings vehicle, such as a money market account, that can provide a decent interest rate *and* easy access to his cash.

Jake should continue to feed this account by having a portion of his pay directly deposited in the account on a biweekly or a monthly basis. With his take home pay at around $5,800 per month (after his 401(k) contributions), he should have plenty of room to save. Even if his living expenses accounted for 50 percent of his income, Jake would have close to $2,000 left over each month to dedicate to saving for specific life expenses.

"These are all moves that Jake can do on his own at first," says Kramer. As he gets older and builds his net worth, perhaps once he has between $250,000 and $500,000 in investable assets, he may want to look for some help from a financial advisor.

For now, Jake needs to educate himself so he can become more confident with his investments and implement basic savings tactics and behaviors. The more he knows and the more he plans now, the more he'll have later.

CHAPTER 7

On Your Own: Individual Retirement Accounts

I went to high school and college with a lot of rich kids. Actually, it's more accurate to say that I went to high school and college with a lot of kids who had rich parents.

But on the surface you would never know the difference.

In high school it was the brand new BMW on your 17th birthday. Leather seats. A car phone. And if that wasn't enough, maybe you also had some custom rims slapped on to make it stand out from the others in the senior parking lot.

In college, it became the all-expenses-paid spring break to Wherever You Like. Cancun. The Bahamas. Acapulco. Kenya. No problem, you're only young once.

I couldn't wait to see where the gift-giving-to-accomplishment ratio would go when I graduated from college in the spring 1999. At the rates I had observed, I expected at least one of my friends to get a small island in the Pacific to commemorate their four years of excess and debauchery.

Some got newer new cars, others trips to Europe. None of the gifts stood out. They were relatively unremarkable, just a continuation of the status quo, and they all seemed to blend together.

Except for one.

A friend, one on the periphery of my core group, was telling me that his parents set him up with an IRA for his graduation. He called it an "Ira." I thought he meant some robotic servant that would do his laundry and cook his meals if and when he grew too lazy.

Of course, I was mistaken. He wasn't embarrassed or proud to tell me about the gift, he was just matter-of-fact.

To me, however, the gift was anything but matter-of-fact. I thought it was ludicrous. I laughed. I thought it was like George Costanza's gifts to the "Human Fund" on *Seinfeld*.

He didn't bother to convince me that it was a decent gift. He didn't crunch any numbers to persuade or impress me.

He didn't bother to tell me that if he had $2,000 sitting in an IRA at the age of 21, that money alone could be worth almost $100,000 when he turns 65.

I didn't realize that this gift, no matter how underwhelming it seemed at the time, was really the only gift that would keep on giving.

And giving.

And giving . . .

———————

You don't have to rely on an employer (or your parents) to start saving money for your retirement. Working for someone else isn't for everybody, so whether you're an actor, waiter, writer, musician, chef, personal trainer, dog walker or still a student, there is a lot that you can do on your own right now, no matter where you are in your career.

Individual Retirement Accounts (IRAs) are one of the best ways for people in their 20s and 30s to start accumulating wealth. You are eligible to contribute to an IRA the second you start earning *any* amount of income.

You don't have to be employed full-time to open up an IRA. You don't even have to wait until you are a certain age to open up one of these accounts if you are eager to start saving right away. There is no minimum contribution either, one of the main reasons that IRAs should be an attractive proposition at any young age.

Also, IRAs can be a really convenient way to consolidate all of your retirement savings as you move from one job to the next. Having an IRA gives you the option to rollover money from work-sponsored retirement plans and maintain your compounding power throughout your working life.

The ability to do these types of rollovers is the main reason that IRAs have grown to become the largest single source for retirement savings, ahead of even the 401(k).

There is more money held in IRAs—$3.67 trillion at the end of 2005, according to the Employee Benefits Research Institute—than 401(k)s plans ($2.97 trillion) or traditional defined benefit pension plans ($2.15 trillion).

These individual retirement accounts are expected to become even more popular and widely used in the near future. Rollovers will continue to fuel IRA growth; but it's also becoming much easier to set these accounts up. You can start an IRA at almost any bank, brokerage, or mutual fund company. And you don't even have to get up off of your couch. You can set up an IRA online if you don't have the time (or the desire) to physically visit any of these kinds of financial institutions.

There is only one requirement to open up an IRA: You have to have some sort of legitimate income. That's it. There are other restrictions depending on the kind of IRA you would like to open. But so long as you are making money, you're eligible to put money into an IRA.

There are a number of different types of IRAs (11 to be exact), but you will mainly want to learn about the Traditional and the Roth IRAs.

The IRS does a great job of breaking down into English the differences between the Roth and the Traditional IRAs in its Publication 590.[1] But as clear as it may be, it's still a 104-page document from an organization solely focused on taxation. I'll give you the rundown and the highlights that matter most to you.

Both the Roth and Traditional IRAs are designed to help you accumulate wealth with the specific goal of retirement in mind. So long as you generally wait until you turn 59.5 years old to take out your money, you will be entitled to a number of tax advantages that will help your money grow more than it would in any kind of standard, taxable savings account. (There are ways to tap into your IRA before you turn 59.5 without being penalized. We get into that later in this chapter. Don't worry, your IRA is always there for you if you need it.)

Both types of IRAs allow you to invest in stocks, bonds, mutual funds, money markets, CDs, or even real estate. Whatever your preference is, you can chose to invest your IRA in almost any type of underlying security. This kind of flexibility is another great feature of the IRA. You don't have to research, buy, and sell individual stocks like a day trader (unless you want to). You can set up your IRA to invest in professionally managed funds, so all you have to do is make contributions. And, at a young age, making your contributions is more important than trying to beat the markets.

Right now you can put up to $4,000 every year in both the Traditional and Roth IRAs. In 2008, the contribution limit will rise to $5,000. This may not sound like a lot at first, especially when you consider that you may need hundreds of thousands—and maybe even millions—of dollars to retire. But when you consider the power of compounding that will be at work here, plus some of the tax benefits that IRAs can provide you with along the way, even small contributions can make a huge difference over the long term.

Consider this basic growth nugget: If you open up either a Traditional or Roth IRA when you are 21 years old and you contribute $1,000 for the next 40 years, your account could be worth roughly $228,000 when you turn 61 assuming average compounded returns of 7 percent.

Your growth potential isn't impacted by your decision to go for either a Traditional or Roth IRA. The major difference between the two is that the Roth lets you keep this *full* amount when you retire. With a Traditional IRA, any money you take out after you turn 59.5 is taxed as income. We'll get into the differences a bit more in a minute; but first it's important to have a general understanding of how much an IRA can do for you.

Let's get back to the last example for one second: 40 years later and you're staring at an IRA worth almost one-quarter of a million dollars. All it took was $1,000 a year that you contributed to yourself. Or you could even look at it as $19.23 a week if that is easier to digest.

No matter how you internalize it, your diligence has just turned into a couple of hundred thousand dollars. You started young, sacrificed a little, and earned a lot.

But let's just say you waited. Instead of starting it at 21, you delayed your decision until you turned 40 to open that same IRA with $1,000 a year and got the same returns.

You would instead be looking at an IRA worth around $48,000 when you turned 61.

That is a difference of roughly $180,000 in the long run. The numbers speak for themselves. The earlier you start the better.

If you are a full-time or a part-time worker, or if you are a freelancer or aspiring entrepreneur, an IRA can be a great way for you to start saving money right now and accumulate the wealth you will need during your retirement. Again, you don't need to wait for somebody to present you with an option to start saving for your retirement. The options are already out there for you right now.

Even if you have a work-sponsored retirement plan, it makes sense to also add an IRA to your retirement savings mix.

Many financial advisors agree that the combination of an IRA with a 401(k) is a rock solid way for someone in their 20s and 30s to build a sufficient foundation for their retirement. And it's not just because both will provide you with dual forms of income during retirement. You can use these accounts along the way to retirement if you need money for things such as the purchase of your first home or to help pay for your children's education. Starting an IRA early on is a great way to play the retirement card; but it also gives you a backup plan when you're saving up for either of these major life expenses. You're committing to retirement, but an IRA also gives you a number of options and more financial flexibility in the immediate future.

These are just a handful or reasons that IRAs are one of the major advantages that we have over previous generations in planning for our retirement. The Roth IRA, one of the best retirement options for a young working person, only first became available in 1998 following some sweeping changes to pension and retirement laws. The Traditional IRA is almost 25 years older and was hatched by the late President Gerald Ford to help workers who were without pensions to save for their retirement.

There is, ultimately, a reason that there are more and more new options now available to help us account for our own retirements— the federal government can't take care of us all. They are, however, going to give us incentives, specifically in the form of tax breaks, to motivate us to take responsibility for funding our own retirements. So long as we wait until we actually retire to take the money out, we will reap the benefits of IRAs and similar kinds of accounts.

However, the only way IRAs help us to be more financially secure in our retirements than previous generations *is if we elect to take advantage of them early enough.*

Ultimately, it is 100 percent your decision to opt in to one of these individual retirement accounts. No one is going to force you to open an IRA.

The choice is ours.

Now you just have to choose.

Roth versus Traditional?

Before we get into which one may be the most appropriate choice for you, it's important to understand the major differences between the two.

- Your contributions to a Traditional IRA can be tax deductible.
- Your contributions to a Roth IRA are never tax deductible.

If you earn $50,000 a year and contribute $4,000 to a Traditional IRA, you can deduct that amount and lower your taxable income to $46,000.

With a Roth, you could contribute that same $4,000 yet you would still be taxed on your $50,000 salary. You cannot deduct your contributions. But here's the trade-off:

- With a Traditional IRA, your money will grow tax-*deferred*, which means you will pay taxes on your withdrawals after you turn 59.5. Money you draw from your Traditional IRA during your retirement will be treated just like regular income.
- With a Roth IRA, you will not pay taxes on any of the money you withdraw from your account after you turn 59.5. It's tax-*free*. You keep every penny.

The Traditional IRA provides you with some pretty nice saving incentives in the short term. You could get a decent break on your taxes every year that you make a contribution; and your contributions, as well as the interest it earns, will grow tax-deferred over time.

But in the end, you will get hit with taxes. And the money you have saved, as well as the earnings your investments have generated, will not be all yours. The idea with the Traditional IRA is that, theoretically, you should be in a lower tax bracket when you are retired, compared with the tax bracket you were in when you were working and making contributions.

With the Roth, you are not getting any immediate tax rewards, but both your contributions and the investment income you earn will also grow without being taxed. Because you are using money from your income, which has already been taxed, you are now done with your IRA taxes.

The younger you are, in theory, the lower your tax bracket should be, which means you might not get tremendous short-term benefits by contributing to a traditional IRA. The major benefit of the Roth is that when you get to the end of the road, or 59.5 years old, every penny in your account belongs to you and no one else.

One way or another, over the course of your working life and your retired life, you are going to pay taxes. You have no idea what kind of tax bracket you will be in later in life, and you have no idea what the federal government will do with tax rates over the next 30 or 40 years.

So here's what you ultimately need to know about the Traditional versus Roth question: When you retire, the only way you will get as much money from a Traditional IRA as you would a Roth, is if you contributed *more money* to the Traditional IRA over the course of your life. Simple as that. You will have to save more along the way to net the same retirement income that you would get from the Roth.

And when you are retired and not working, you will need all the income you can get. While there are no guarantees in life, there is a pretty good chance that you will need the money later in life more than you will need it now, in your youngest working years.

With a Roth, there are no surprises at the end, all of the guesswork was taken care of when you made your contributions and paid your taxes along the way. When you retire, it will be all yours, no matter what.

Most advisors and financial planners say that the younger you are, the more sense it makes for you to choose a Roth over a Traditional IRA. "The Roth is one of the most outstanding savings vehicles to ever happen to young people," says Georgia Bruggeman, chief investment advisor and founder of Median Financial Advisors in Holliston, Massachusetts.

And Bruggeman points out that the earlier you start, the more outstanding your Roth can be.

Consider the example we used earlier of a 25-year-old who decided to contribute $4,000 a year to a Roth IRA for the next 40 years. He'll have $1.1 million in his Roth waiting for him when he turns 65 if he earned an average compounded return of 8 percent over the years. That $1.1 million is all his the day he turns 59.5. He won't be taxed on a cent of that total when he starts making his withdrawals.

If he had decided to open a Traditional IRA instead of a Roth and had the same returns, he'd also be looking at the same amount of $1.1 million when he turns 65. Again, we're assuming that the underlying investments are the same so the returns wouldn't change. But he would have to pay taxes on the withdrawals; and if you assumed that he'd pay a tax rate of 15 percent on the distributions he takes from his Traditional IRA during the course of his retirement, he would have been looking at paying roughly $300,000 in income taxes off of the $1.1 million he accumulated in his IRA.

Over the course of his working life, he would have lowered his taxable income by $160,000. During his retirement, however, he could be paying out $300,000 in taxes. In its simplest form, the Traditional IRA is a bet. You're guessing (or hoping) that you will be in a lower tax bracket when you retire than you were when you were actually working. Consider your age and consider your income levels. Also consider other types of retirement savings you have. The 401(k), for example, is the same concept as a traditional IRA: an incentive to save via tax-deferred growth. At the end of the road, your 401(k) withdrawals will be taxed as income when you use it for your retirement.

Then consider the short-term benefits of lowering your taxable income. The younger you are, the more sense a Roth may make because you will sacrifice a little now to have a lot more later.

"It's tough to make an argument to open a Traditional IRA when you are young," says Scott Cole, founder and principal of Cole Financial Planning in Bessemer, Alabama. "The Roth is less restrictive and has a lot more to offer."

Now You Know the Difference, But What Are You Entitled to?

There is more to consider here than just the taxes, however.

You may make too much money to be eligible for a Roth. Or, if you are already using a work-sponsored retirement plan, you may not be able to deduct all of your contributions to a Traditional IRA.

The IRS is willing to help us out, but they aren't necessarily going to make it easy.

Before you can make a choice between a Roth or a Traditional IRA, you need to figure out how your current earnings and benefits could impact your ability to choose between the two.

While the Roth may be the best IRA option in your youngest years, if you earn too much money, you are not going to be allowed to make contributions.

If your "adjusted growth income" is less than $99,000 in 2007, then no worries. (Your adjusted growth income is right at the bottom of the first page on your 1040 forms that you use to file your taxes. I hate taxes, believe me, but it's important to know what you are really earning, reporting and able to deduct in any given year.)

If you earn more than $99,000, you may run into some issues with the Roth. The maximum compensation levels will change over the years, but let's stick with the 2007 rules for now. Here's the deal:

- For 2007, if you alone earn more than $114,000 in a year, you can't contribute to a Roth in that year *at all*.
- There is also a compensation cutoff for married couples who jointly file their taxes. If together you both earn more than $166,000 in a given year, then it's the same deal. Neither spouse is permitted to make a contribution to a Roth that year.

Even if you already have a Roth that you've been contributing to, it's off-limits when you're earning above the maximum allowable compensation levels. (By the way, if you already have a Roth and you cross the maximum compensation mark, *only* your ability to contribute is affected. The IRS will not force you to close your IRA or liquidate your account. No matter how much your compensation may increase over the years, the money you have contributed to a Roth is always there.)

If you happen to fall in between $99,000 and $114,000 as an individual, or $156,000 and $166,000 as a couple, you are in a bit of a gray area. The Roth is not totally off-limits, but you cannot make the maximum contributions. If you are a 'tweener, then there is a phase-out (an IRS term, not mine) rule that applies. Here's how it works:

- Figure out how much money you have earned above the $99,000 mark and below the $114,000 mark. Let's make it easy and say you made $106,500 last year, *exactly in the middle* of the in-between zone. That means you can make *half* of the $4,000 maximum contribution.
- If you were making $102,750 dollars, then you would be 25 percent above the $99,000 threshold. That means you reduce the maximum contribution of $4,000, by 25 percent. So you could contribute $3,000 to your Roth, rather than $4,000.

- Ultimately, there is a window here—either $15,000 for an individual or $10,000 for a married couple. Figure out the portion of that window that your excess salary represents. Subtract that from the maximum contribution.
- Move on with your life. Go do something fun.

Roth IRA's were originally designed to help "middle class" workers to save for retirement, hence the maximum compensation limits. This makes it even more important for you to start your Roth at the earliest age possible.

Theoretically, your compensation should be at its lowest levels in your earliest working years. Ideally it will increase over time, so it's critical to contribute to your Roth before you make too much money and you are no longer qualified to make contributions.

Even if you can only contribute for a handful of years in your 20s, you will have set yourself up with a nice little retirement stash.

For example, say you started contributing $4,000 a year at the age of 25 to your Roth IRA and then at the age of 30 you earned too much money to qualify to make the maximum contributions.

If you never became eligible to contribute to your Roth again after the age of 30, those six years of contributions would be worth $217,000 when you turn 60 (assuming an average compounded annual return of 7 percent).

And let's just say you decide to wait until you turn 65 before you touch your Roth. You're looking at $305,000.

With six years of contributions totaling $24,000, you have put yourself in a position to generate a significant amount of financial security later in life. And every last penny of that money is yours with the Roth. You won't pay taxes on a dime when you start withdrawing, so long as you play by the IRS's rules and wait until you turn 59.5 to start taking your money out.

Also, just to illustrate the power of your youth that's at work here, let's stick with this example. Your six years of maximum IRA contributions from ages 25 to 30 could be worth $217,000 at the age of 60. But what if you waited?

What if you waited until the age of 42 to start making contributions? If you started contributing $4,000 *every year* until you turned 60 (still assuming 7 percent returns) your Roth would be worth about $150,000.

You have contributed more money and you will still walk away with a significantly smaller account value.

At 42, you will contribute a total of $72,000 over 18 years for your Roth to be worth $150,000 when you turn 60.

At 25, you will contribute $24,000 over six years for your account to be worth $217,000 when you turn 60.

This doesn't even consider that you will have a lot of life expenses in your 40s that do not exist in your 20s. You will have to contribute more when you may have less available.

You shouldn't even have to consider that—just look at the numbers. You don't have to be Einstein to recognize that compounding can be the most powerful force in *your* universe.

Traditional IRAs Limitations

Unlike the Roth, with a Traditional IRA you are always eligible to make contributions as long as you are earning any kind of legitimate income. No matter what you are earning—even if you pull in $500,000 or $1 million in a year—you can still pump money into a Traditional IRA.

But with the Traditional IRA, you may not always be eligible to take advantage of its greatest perk: your ability to deduct your contributions to your taxes.

If you are covered by a work-sponsored retirement plan, such as a 401(k), then you need to pay attention. If you are not, then you can always deduct your IRA contributions from your taxes annually.

But if you're participating in a 401(k), there are some pretty strict rules that the IRS has put out about who can fully enjoy all of the Traditional IRA's best features.

If you are already in a retirement plan at work, for 2007, you cannot deduct your Traditional IRA contribution if:

- You, as a single person, earn more than $62,000 in that year.
- Earn more than $103,000 as a couple filing taxes jointly.

But wait, there's more. If you are not covered by a retirement plan at work, but your spouse is, you cannot deduct your Traditional IRA contributions if together, you jointly earn more than $166,000 during the 2007 tax year.

In any of these situations, you can still contribute to a Traditional IRA. You just are not eligible to deduct your contributions from your taxes. Also it does not matter how much or how little you have in your retirement plan at work. Only your compensation is relevant here.

Lastly, there is also an "in-between" stage that will allow you to deduct at least part of your contributions. If you are in a work-sponsored plan, your Traditional IRA contributions are partially deductible if:

- You alone earn between $52,000 and $62,000.
- As a couple filing taxes jointly you earn between $83,000 and $103,000.

If you're not covered by a work plan, but your spouse is, you can deduct part of your Traditional IRA contributions if together you earn between $156,000 and $166,000.

These compensation levels will change over time. But as of 2007, if you earn less than $52,000 as an individual, or less than $83,000 as a couple filing jointly in the 2007 tax year, then these rules don't apply to you even if you're covered in a work-sponsored plan.

Why do you need to know all this? These details can all seem pretty hairy, but before you can make a good decision on an IRA you need to know all of the facts.

Remember, if you are offered a retirement plan at work and your employer will match any or all of your contributions to the plan, this should be your first move. Free money = No brainer.

If you are already taking advantage of a work-sponsored retirement plan, then this may make the Roth even more appropriate for you in your 20s or 30s.

You want to be able maximize all of the incentives you are being offered. You want your money to be running on all cylinders.

So if you have a work plan and you earn too much to deduct your contributions, the Traditional IRA becomes less attractive. Your money still grows tax-deferred over the years; but you won't be getting tax benefits in either the short term or the long term if you don't qualify for the tax-deductibility perk. You will get taxed on your full income now and you will get taxed later on the income you withdraw from your IRA during retirement.

With the Roth, you have a larger window of opportunity. You are qualified to contribute until you earn up to six-figures, even if you participate in a retirement plan at work. And no matter what, the money you accumulate in your Roth will always be tax-free when you take it out for your retirement. And you always will have the option to do *both*. If you start out with a Roth and then you earn too much to keep contributing, you can then open up a Traditional IRA. If you can deduct the contributions, you will be getting a bigger break on your taxes at that point because you are earning more.

If this is not compelling enough, there are a few other perks that make the Roth a more appropriate option over a Traditional IRA when you are young.

For starters, if you need to access any of the money you have saved *before you retire*, the Roth IRA is much more friendly than the Traditional IRA.

With a Roth, you can withdraw your contributions at any time without paying any penalties and without paying any taxes. This is one of the best features of a Roth for a young person, points out Marvin Rotenberg, the director of individual retirement services at Bank of America. This kind of "flexibility" can be indispensable for a younger person over the course of a lifetime.

The idea is to leave your money in your IRA until your retire, so try to avoid using it as a savings account. But there may come a time that you need cash, and you can always access your *contributions* to a Roth without any consequences whatsoever.

You cannot, however, take out more than you have contributed to your Roth without paying a penalty. You will pay taxes and a 10 percent penalty if you withdraw any of the earnings in your Roth. So, for example, if you have contributed $40,000 to your Roth, yet it grows to become worth $65,000 including the interest your investments have earned, you can take out up to $40,000 without getting slapped with a fee or taxes. Withdraw a penny more and you will pay the price.

There are two exceptions, however, that allow you to take out both your contributions and your earnings—both can be relevant when you are in your 20s and 30s:

- If you are buying your first home then you can take up to $10,000 out from your Roth IRA, including earnings. No penalties and no taxes will apply. So, if you have contributed $8,000 but your account is now at $10,000, you can take it all out so long as you are going to put the money towards the purchase of your first home. That's tax-free earnings that you are entitled to with this exception. Also, if you have a spouse, he or she can take out $10,000 as well, so you can use a total of $20,000 in Roth savings in this situation. And, just so you know, "first home" doesn't technically have to be your first home. If you haven't owned a home in two years, then it somehow qualifies as a first home in the eyes of the IRS. To enjoy this perk, your Roth must be open for at least five years; otherwise you will pay taxes on the withdrawal.
- If you are putting the money towards your kid's college, then you can take out money from your Roth and you will not have to pay taxes on any earnings you withdraw. You will, however, have to pay the 10 percent early withdrawal penalty if you take out more than you contributed. But again, the earnings you take out are tax-free if the money goes towards funding your child's education.

In a lot of ways, the Roth can be a nice hedge between saving for retirement and saving for a house or your kid's education. Because you can start a Roth at any age, the earlier you start, the more options you will have down the road. Ideally, financial planners suggest that you also set up set up separate accounts to save for housing and education, but it's not always that easy to be saving in multiple directions. Again, remember, you can take out loans to help pay for almost anything in this world, *but you will not be able to take out a loan to cover the cost of your retirement.*

If you do choose to take money out of your Roth, unlike taking out a loan from your 401(k), you don't pay it back. So just remember, every time you subtract money, you are impairing both your account balance and your compounding power. It's always good to think of your Roth as a last resort, but it's also comforting to know that the money's there for you if or when you may really need it later in life.

With a Traditional IRA, there is not a lot of flexibility when it comes to early withdrawals. You will be taxed on early withdrawals because you have to report it as income. You will also usually have to pay a 10 percent early withdrawal penalty as well, unless you're putting the money withdrawn towards one of the IRS's eight early distribution exceptions:

1. You're disabled.
2. You're buying, building or repairing your first home.
3. The withdrawals are not more than the cost of your medical insurance.
4. You have unreimbursed medical expenses that are more than 7.5 percent of your income.
5. Your early withdrawals are not more than your qualified higher education expenses.
6. You are the beneficiary of a deceased IRA owner.
7. You need the money because of an IRS levy.
8. You take the money in an annuity.

Flexibility Now and Flexibility Later

There is one last feature of the Roth IRA that is important to note too. The Roth is also a more flexible account when you are retired, compared with the Traditional IRA.

This may be a long way away, but it's one of the Roth's most attractive features. When you have a Traditional IRA, you are required to start taking distributions from the account when you turn 70.5. You also can't make any additional contributions to a Traditional IRA after you turn 70.5.

With a Roth, however, you are never required to start taking money out. It can sit for as long as you like. And you can even continue to make contributions to your Roth during your retirement if you are still earning an income. It's up to you. With the Roth, *you* make the calls.

Great, I'm Convinced. Now Where Do I Get an IRA?

You can generally open up at IRA with any bank, brokerage house, or mutual fund company. You can even open it up online if you like.

But call me Old School. I still like to do it in-person because I will always have questions. I don't care how annoying my questions may be, I deserve answers. Never be afraid to ask a question, no matter how dumb you think it might be.

Where you go to open up your account really depends on how you want to invest your IRA. If you want your IRA money to go into more conservative banking investments, like CDs or money markets, then go to a bank.

Your bank can also set your IRA up to invest in mutual funds if that's your preference, or you can always go directly to a mutual fund company to set your IRA up with them. If you want to invest your IRA directly into individual stocks that you can pick on your own, then go to a broker.

Any financial planner or adviser you talk to will tell you that early on you shouldn't be putting your money in ultraconservative investments such as money market accounts or bonds. Save these investments for later in life when you need to preserve your money and invest in things that will generate a steady income for you.

For now, you need to focus on making your money grow; this makes stocks or equities—the terms are interchangeable—a more appropriate option for younger investors than, say, bonds, because stocks have historically proven to have more long-term growth potential.

If you don't know anything about picking stocks, then mutual funds are a solid choice for your IRA because they will select a mix of stocks on your behalf. If you do know a thing or two about choosing stocks, then mutual funds may still be a good choice because you will be leaving your money to professional investors and you don't have to take the time (or risks) to manage your own retirement money.

Ultimately, try and find a fund that is low-cost and mimics a major stock market index—this is an easy way to get broad exposure to multiple stocks without taking on too much concentrated risk.

This is why you may also want to consider exchange-traded funds for your IRA. These funds, which are cleverly referred to as ETFs, are very similar in concept to mutual funds because they invest in a basket of specific securities. A specific ETF will generally track an index, much like a passive mutual fund. The main difference is that ETFs are listed on exchanges, which means they trade throughout the day just like an individual stock.

ETFs also tend to have cheaper costs associated with them than mutual funds, which makes them a smart option for your IRA as well.

Try to keep your costs down as much as possible. Remember, the fees and commissions you pay for financial services companies to run your money will ultimately subtract from the investment returns that they give you. There is no way to avoid paying some sort of fees or commissions for certain financial services. You are ultimately paying for a service; you are paying for someone else to maximize your retirement savings potential.

Once you figure out exactly where to point your IRA money, all you will have to do after that is continue to make contributions. "It doesn't have to be rocket science," says Eddie Kramer, the financial planner with Abacus Planning Group who weighed in on Jake's retirement options in the previous chapter. "When you're young, the most important thing to focus on is getting in the habit of saving and starting to accumulate wealth."

Just to make it even easier on yourself, set up a direct deposit function to fund your IRA contributions. I opened up my Roth with my bank and I now have $333.33 taken out of my checking account once a month and it is directly deposited into my Roth IRA.

Rather than writing one check for $4,000, I convinced myself that it was necessary for me to divide that contribution up over the course of the year. Not only does this prevent me from spending the money, but it also takes any decisionmaking out of the process. If I ever thought I had an "extra" $4,000 sitting around, I'd be on a beach in St. Martin in six weeks or less. No questions asked.

I may still be young, but I know myself well enough by now. I need to be on autopilot. One rational decision may just be enough to save me from dozens of impulsive mistakes.

Rollovers: Making the Case for a Traditional IRA

While the Roth should be your first choice when you are in your early working years, there will likely be a role for a Traditional IRA later in life. Specifically, when you change jobs, you will want to consider using a Traditional IRA.

If you have been participating in a 401(k), you can take this money with you when you change jobs. You will have to decide what you want to do with this money when you leave, which is where the Traditional IRA comes into play.

The money you have accumulated in your 401(k) came from your gross pay, so these are dollars that have not been taxed. You want it to stay that way, believe me, otherwise you will have to pay some pretty hefty taxes if you just take out your 401(k) money in a lump sum and don't do a rollover. You're also deflating your compounding power so please do not take a lump sum payout, no matter how little may be in your account.

If you do a rollover to a Traditional IRA, you can transfer your entire 401(k) balance into the account and it will continue to grow tax-deferred until your retirement—just as it would have if it stayed in the 401(k). And, if you change your job again, you can always rollover any new 401(k) assets into this same Traditional IRA account. It's an effective way to consolidate all of your old retirement savings and maintain all of your tax advantages and compounding power.

So, even if you already have a Roth IRA, there is also a specific place for a Traditional IRA in your life as well. You cannot do a direct rollover from your 401(k) into a Roth IRA. Remember, you have funded your Roth with aftertax dollars and it is a tax-free savings vehicle. You cannot mix and match without paying the price.

You could rollover your 401(k) into a Traditional IRA and then do a "recharacterization" to move the money into your Roth. This simply means that you will have to report this money as income for that year. So if your 401(k) balance was $25,000, you would be taxed on an additional $25,000 of income when you do a recharacterization. Long story short: It's not a good idea.

If you don't rollover your money into an IRA, you may be able to keep it with your former employer or roll it over into your new 401(k). Again, the IRA is a better move because you will have more investment options. You don't just have to stick with the 10 to 20 funds that your employer has offered. With an IRA, you can invest your money in almost anything you want.

IRAs are easy to set up and rollovers are not complicated transactions—but they are formal transactions that require some actual paperwork. You can't just take the cash and then eventually park it in an IRA. That's not a rollover, believe me. That simple mistake cost me roughly almost $3,000 in taxes and early withdrawal fees when I thought I could roll the money over to an IRA on my own.

A rollover requires your former employer (or your former plan administrator) to formally communicate with the financial institution that is providing you with the IRA.

Before you can initiate a rollover, you have to set up your IRA (if you do not have an IRA already). You don't need to put any money in this account, you just need to establish the account and get the account number. In most cases, you can do this online, over the phone, or in person at a branch of any bank, mutual fund company or brokerage.

Then you have to tell your employer or administrator that you are rolling your 401(k) money into an IRA. This is where the paperwork comes in; you will probably have to complete some distribution forms so you properly steer the money into the IRA you have just opened; in some cases, the financial institution providing you with the IRA may actually do this work for you, it just depends on your provider. This communication will allow you to avoid any early withdrawal penalties and taxes. Basically, they are now writing the check to a financial institution, not you.

Be sure to ask your employer, or whoever is cutting your distribution check, how long the rollover should take. Every employer is different and some take longer than others to complete the transaction. But you can always call your former employer, or even check the status of your rollover online wherever you have opened up the IRA, to get an update.

It's just a two-step process. All you have to do is open the IRA and direct the distribution to your new account. No more, no less. While cashing out of your 401(k) when you move on may seem like the easiest option, it's also the worst move you can make. Roll it over, keep your money, and most importantly—keep it growing.

CHAPTER 8

Taking the Heat to Stay in His Kitchen

Brian works more hours than a new lawyer and sweats more than a construction worker. Problem is, after nine years of grinding it out as a cook in four different cities, he still makes less than he would have if he had taken an entry-level corporate gig right out of school.

Money has never meant much to Brian, 30, which is a good thing because he has never saved a penny. Ever.

But he thinks it's a fair trade-off. He wants and needs experience more than anything else; he can't just claim to be a chef, he has to be a chef. And if that means he barely gets by until he can open up his own restaurant, then he could care less. He's doing what he has always loved. "You couldn't persuade me with any amount of money to deal with a life of water coolers, 401(k)s or fluorescents," says Brian. "There's nothing in that for me. I'm doing the only thing I could ever consider doing."

He's single, now living in San Francisco, running the kitchen at a well-known eatery in the Castro District. He has a love-hate relationship with this job, much like every other job he has had.

Now he's starting to see the light. Hopefully, he says, he's at the tail end of paying his dues. He finally became a salaried worker last year, earning himself an annual salary of close to $40,000 a year—not enough to live too comfortably in San Francisco, but still nearly double what he took home the year before when he was only getting paid by the hour.

By becoming a salaried employee last year, Brian was also introduced to another concept that he's never been offered at work before: health insurance. He had been paying out-of-pocket (or not-at-all) for health insurance since he graduated college. If ever he wanted a workplace benefit, this was certainly his preferred perk.

Health insurance has been a reach for years, so the idea of having any kind of retirement plan sounds almost crazy to Brian. Not only has he not been eligible for one at any of his previous jobs, he couldn't attempt to find the money to put away for his retirement even if he wanted to. Last year, he had to sell his car and start taking the bus just to breathe a little easier every month. Right now he needs money for almost everything but retirement.

He confesses that one day he might like to be retired. But he hasn't given much thought about how he will support himself financially 30 years from now. Living debt-free at this very moment, he adds, is enough of a challenge.

He's had a bad history with credit cards dating back to his early college years, when he racked up almost $20,000 in debt. The only way he ever got out from under that debt was by selling "massive quantities" of marijuana for a year, something Brian is both proud and ashamed of. "It was an option. It wasn't the best or the worst option, but it worked," he says. "I always thought that it was criminal what the credit card companies were doing to me, so I had no problem doing something criminal to get them off of my back."

Brian's ability to rationalize so clearly might have been what got him into debt in the first place—something he admits. It also might be why he doesn't see the need to save right now. His father owns a successful small business on the East Coast and one day Brian thinks he will inherit a small fortune that could take care of his debts or set him up for his retirement. "I have always kind of known that there's a Plan B if I don't get it right," he says. "I don't know if I'm lucky or stupid to think that way, but I can't help it."

Right now, however, he says he's most focused on his Plan A. He needs to make his restaurant happen. He's not married, he has no kids, and he's only responsible for himself; there's no better time to take a chance, he says.

When he's done working back-to-back shifts now, he goes home and he works on his business plan. Sometimes he scouts out locations; other times he's putting together dinner parties for friends,

friends-of-friends, and hopefully some future investors in his restaurant. He's been doing this for the last year, knowing that he needs to sell himself. "Every conversation can be an opportunity," he says, without sounding the slightest bit slippery.

While he hasn't managed to save a penny for himself, he has corralled a small group of individual investors who have verbally agreed to back his restaurant with close to $400,000 in silent capital. That hasn't helped his savings psyche much either, he adds.

But now he knows he's about to make the great leap soon. If he can't get his restaurant off the ground in the next 18 to 24 months, he says he'll consider himself a failure. And even if Brian does get his business up-and-running, he knows that he is not guaranteed to be successful right away.

Or ever.

He won't know until he knows. Every hour he's worked and every dish he's cooked over the last nine years has had a purpose. He's stopped just dreaming out loud. Now he thinks, he plans, he acts. He says he is ready.

He has paid all of his dues *today* with his mind's eye staring at *tomorrow*. Oddly enough, while he's always taken time to tend to his dream, he's never stopped to take care of himself. "Everything has a way of taking care of itself," he says.

"I think," he says.

"I hope," he follows.

"We'll see."

Prescription

First things first—Brian needs to forget about the possibility of an inheritance. If he doesn't get it, he'll have to play catch-up for the rest of his life. He may also inherit less than he expects, which financial planners say happens fairly often. "Those types of things are taboo to talk about," says Jeff Zures, cofounder Sanchez & Zures LLC, a McLean, Virginia-based financial planning firm. "But unfortunately they're not necessarily taboo to think about."

In looking at Brian's situation, Zures knows it is way too risky for Brian, or anyone for that matter, to ignore the need to save today because he expects to cash in on some sort of windfall later. The best thing he can do right now is forget about the possibilities and start his own reality.

Brian may not have a work-sponsored retirement plan, and he might not have much spare cash either, especially living in a costly city like San Francisco. But he is not entirely without options. For starters, Zures recommends that Brian opens up a Roth IRA and begins making monthly contributions to the account—preferably getting the monthly contributions either directly deposited into his IRA by his employer, or by having his bank set up a recurring transfer from his checking account to his Roth.

"Even if it's as little as $20 a month at first, it will still help him get in the habit of saving for his retirement, and hopefully change his mind-set a bit," says Zures. Over time, he adds, Brian should begin to increase his monthly contributions to his Roth, ideally every time he gets a pay raise. Or, if there is ever a case where he receives a bonus or does some extra work on the side, Brian should put this money straight into his Roth, with a goal of contributing the maximum of $4,000.

The Roth will also give Brian some flexibility as he moves forward in life. "The money isn't gone or locked up for the next 30 or 40 years. When he goes to buy his first house, for example, he can always tap his Roth if he needs more money," says Cary Carbonaro, a certified financial planner at Family Financial Research in Lake County, Florida. "It will allow him to play two hands at once. I'd even tell him to start his Roth before he starts an emergency fund."

Fortunately, Brian doesn't have serious issues with debt anymore, which means he can focus on saving money and building for his future. Given Carbonaro's viewpoint, Brian should commit to a basic budget and ultimately aim to put away $100 a month at first. "You have to be realistic," says Carbonaro. "If you can't do the maximum, anything is better than nothing. And he still has enough time to accumulate some wealth."

Aside from the Roth, Brian may also want to consider investing directly in a mutual fund, according to Scott Cole, founder and principal of Cole Financial Planning in Bessemer, Alabama.

Cole sees a lifecycle or target-date fund as a good option for Brian because it can be an easy and relatively low-cost way to set up a properly allocated and balanced portfolio. Brain won't have to do much maintenance either. Once he has selected a fund, he should set up a direct deposit or recurring transfer to invest in the fund every month. "He doesn't have access to a 401(k), but he does have the ability to choose any lifecycle or target-date fund he wants and duplicate what he should be doing if he was participating in a retirement plan," says. Cole.

Cole also thinks that as Brian advances on his dream to open up his own restaurant, it will become even more critical for Brain to have personal savings and retirement accounts. "Most entrepreneurs have their net worth tied directly into their business ventures," Cole says. "In his field it's particularly risky to have all of his eggs in one basket. It's a competitive industry and it's also unpredictable, so it's important for him to establish some net worth that is not at all related to his restaurant. If he goes all-in, he is just too vulnerable."

At the moment, Brian has absolutely nothing saved and his restaurant is only a business plan; getting something going, such as the Roth, should be his top priority.

His restaurant may be his biggest asset one day, but his age is his biggest asset right now. Brian needs to make this asset work for him; every day that he does not save is a lost opportunity to secure a piece of his future. In the end, whether it's the inheritance or the restaurant, there is too much riding on possibility as Cole sees Brian at this point. "He needs to establish some stability for himself because he could win just as easily as he could lose."

CHAPTER 9

You Are Not on Your Own

HELP HAS ARRIVED. FINALLY

I obsess over fantasy basketball.

I can't help it. I don't want to know so much about basketball—I *need* to know. I can't stand the thought of not knowing something that other people might already know.

I subscribe to ridiculous websites to get information that I think might give me an edge over the other degenerate NBA fans in my league (who also subscribe to the same ridiculous websites for the same information).

I listen to fake experts analyze the same games that I have already watched in the hopes that they can tell me that they saw something that I didn't see.

I believe deep down in my stomach that there is a system to be had here, a fantasy basketball *matrix*, that when I discover it, will prevent me from ever losing.

I will crack the code and I will be invincible.

I just haven't figured it out yet.

But I'm sure I will.

One day.

I think.

I hope.

Until then, I'll just continue to consume an inordinate amount of information. I will continue to talk about basketball with anyone who will listen or entertain my rants.

And I will continue to produce only average results.

I'm not telling you any of this just to get it off my chest, no matter how good it feels to confess.

Maybe you know some people who are equally as infatuated with investing, or the stock market. At the very least, you have probably been subject to a conversation with people who only want to talk about how much money they've made off of a certain penny stock or some hot mutual fund.

If you don't care, that's fine.

But if you feel you are not as well-equipped to invest your money as these other people may be—you are completely mistaken.

There is a lot of financial pornography out there that can make money matters seem much more complicated than they really have to be. They may make you feel like you're missing out on something that everyone else knows but you.

Thousands of people want to teach you how to beat the markets, how to find the next Microsoft, or how to run your money like a billionaire hedge fund manager.

If this is *your* obsession, then go for it; fill up your TiVo with *Mad Money* and stare at MSNBC all day long.

But exposing yourself to all sorts of information does not guarantee that you will make more money off of your investments.

If you did not idolize Alex P. Keaton when you were growing up, that's okay. There are better ways to get decent returns on your investments. You can do it with little more than some basic understanding and discipline.

Do not allow yourself to be intimidated, because this is not an excuse to delay saving money, especially in a retirement plan.

At a young age, the most important investment decision you will make when it comes to saving for your retirement is not what stocks or funds you should buy through your 401(k)—it is whether or not you actually decide to opt in.

There are ways to actually participate in your 401(k), for example, without having to pick out every which way you want to invest your retirement money. So do not be deterred from saving if you think you don't know enough about investing. Most people don't. Even those that think they do, well, it probably doesn't make too much of a difference in the end anyway.

Once you choose to participate at a young age, you're already putting yourself ahead of the game.

When this book was just a dream, I started informally polling friends and friends-of-friends just to find out how, or if, people my own age were saving for their retirement. I heard a lot of different reasons why people were not saving, but I couldn't get over how many people told me that they thought it was too difficult to get started.

I always thought that money, or lack of it, would be the real main reason for not participating. A lot of younger workers use this as an excuse rather than admit what they think is an embarrassing truth.

Saying that you are broke sounds like a legit reason not to participate in a 401(k). But admitting that you don't know what you're doing? That's just admitting that you have no excuse.

I remember talking to one woman in her late 20s who has about 8 percent of her paycheck automatically deposited into her savings account every month. She was eligible for a 401(k) at work, one that would have matched every dollar she contributed for up to 6 percent of her pay. She opted for a standard savings account instead. She knew she was forfeiting free money. She didn't care.

She told me that she wanted to participate but said she ultimately didn't understand her 401(k). She chose not to contribute after she was given the brochure on her retirement plan. There were more than 20 funds that she had to choose from, and she didn't have a clue what she was looking at. She couldn't tell one fund from another—and she didn't want to either. She heard terms like "risk tolerance," "asset allocation," and "rebalancing" and tuned out.

There was too much margin for error, she told me, and she elected for something that she already understood: her bank account.

I couldn't believe it. I still can't believe it. She was *this* close to putting money in her 401(k), but instead she consciously decided to leave more money on the table because she didn't want to be bothered with some of the basic ins-and-outs of investing.

Who could blame her?

It's certainly not that she couldn't understand her 401(k) and do a solid job of maintaining her portfolio. She just didn't want to. She does creative design for an advertising company and she'd rather read *Ad Age* than *Barron's*.

She didn't want to make the wrong choice and she also didn't want to do the standard upkeep—review your funds once a year and then figure out if you have the right mix, or if you should "rebalance."

This just got me thinking more about how people actually chose their investment options in their 401(k)s. I kept asking. I still keep asking.

The average 401(k) plan makes 19 different funds available to participants, according to the Profit Sharing/401k Council of America.

Some people look at all these funds and just decide to choose their own funds randomly and haphazardly. Some seek out help from a friend or family member who works in finance. Some ask a coworker for advice. Some decide to forget the whole thing because they think it's just not for them. And others are so confident in their investing skills that they buy-and-sell funds in their 401(k) as if they were day-trading through a brokerage account.

At the end of the day, what you have is a number of people who have no idea whatsoever how their 401(k) money is invested. Roughly one in every four workers under the age of 30 have absolutely no clue what the money in their 401(k) is doing, according to a Merrill Lynch survey published in June 2005.[1]

It's totally random and totally inefficient. When left to our own devices, younger participants in 401(k)s either have no idea how their 401(k) money is invested, or they are often not making the right decisions.

At a time when we can afford to take the most investment risk, many younger investors actually opt for safer, more conservative investment options that offer limited potential for returns.

It might be a lack of investment confidence, according to Pamela Hess, director of retirement research at Hewitt Associates, who points to a survey the firm did in 2006 of three generations preparing for retirement. But Generation X workers, ages 18 to 25, have almost 35 percent of their 401(k) money invested in bonds, while the Baby Boomers, ages 42 to 59, allocate only about 31 percent to bonds. "Some younger workers may be worried about losing their money," Hess says, "and others just don't know what they're doing." Others may have automatically been defaulted into these investment options by their employer without even knowing.

And that's been the downside to work-sponsored retirement plans like the 401(k). For the most part, you have been on your own. You've had to act like your own financial advisor in many ways, which, for a lot of people isn't easy, let alone prudent. Companies have tried to educate their employees, thinking that this could correct the problem, but in many cases it may have just complicated the issue even further.

There is good news. The system is getting a much-needed make-over prompted by the Pension Protection Act passed in 2006, and we will be the first generation to grow up in a new-and-improved era of workplace retirement plans.

So while it is still your retirement plan and your responsibility, you are no longer entirely on your own.

More and more, employers are starting to offer guidance and give you access to real advice, rather than general education. And, perhaps more importantly, more employers are starting to give you options in your retirement plan that will allow you to "set it and for-get it" if you like. In some cases, you might not have to even choose these options—you may be automatically enrolled in a 401(k) when you start your next job, and your investments may even be put on autopilot (appropriately) the day you are enrolled.

It was only a matter of time. The 401(k) used to just be a supple-ment to traditional pensions when they first came out. The problem is 401(k)s are not just a supplement anymore—they are becoming the workhorses for more and more people's retirement security. They are not just privileged savings accounts for the savvy or the rich who can afford to put away more than the rest of us. They have, in many ways, already become our primary source of future retirement income.

"If it's going to be the dominant retirement vehicle for the masses, it needs to be better designed for the masses," says William Gale, vice president and director of economic studies at the Brook-ings Institution, a think-tank in Washington D.C.

401(k) plans are available to millions of people who may not know, or may not ever care to know, anything about mutual funds, diversification or asset allocation. And, as the 401(k) has become more important to more people, more employers and financial serv-ices companies have recognized that they need to get with the times.

Slowly but surely, the 401(k) system is evolving from a do-it-yourself to a do-it-for me world. If you don't ever want to know anything about investing, that's fine—but now you have some solid all-inclusive options that require you to do next to nothing.

You can choose, for example, one single fund in your 401(k) that will age and change with you over time. Or, if you don't want to make any decisions at all, more employers are introducing programs that will allow you to hand off complete management of your 401(k) to a provider who will run your money on your behalf (and also take your other assets into consideration, too).

Moving away from the system of old is a good thing and younger workers are already approving of these changes. Almost 60 percent of young workers surveyed by Prudential Retirement at the end of 2006 said that "automatic" defined contributions plans are a welcome change, while another 53 percent of younger workers said that they believe they'll get better returns on the 401(k) investments by putting them on autopilot.[2]

"Younger workers don't think that the do-it-yourself model is the best option anymore," says Deanna Garen, senior vice president of strategic planning and development at Prudential Retirement. Some have seen how the older model has failed people from their parent's generations, says Ms. Garen, while other young workers admit that they are either not interested or frightened by the prospect of managing their own 401(k) investments.

Of course, if you would like to be in complete control, you can still choose to run your own 401(k) at your discretion. No one is taking away your ability to be in control; you are now just simply being offered a new of set less-complicated, all-inclusive choices.

It's really up to you, but that's a good thing. You have options. You just need to know what they are.

What You Need: A Quick Investing 101

Most financial advisors will tell you that the key to having long-term investment success can come down to one word: diversity.

This means that your portfolio should have a proper mix of investments, or asset allocation, to protect you when—not if— parts of your portfolio do not perform well. A diverse portfolio will consist of investments in various asset classes, which will almost always include stocks, bonds, and cash, at the most basic level.

The general purpose of asset allocation, ultimately, is to reduce risk. "Managing risk is not the same as avoiding it," says Dr. Peng Chen, president and chief investment officer of Ibbotson Associates, a financial advisory firm in Chicago. "If you are properly diversified at a young age, your investments do not need to be conservative. You can, and should, take more risks."

Theoretically, stocks have unlimited potential for growth. With stocks, you are buying partial ownership in a company. If a company is doing well and is producing strong earnings, the value of its stock will often increase. And ultimately, there is no ceiling on its value. A stock is worth whatever buyers are willing to pay for it.

At the same time, however, stocks also can be very volatile and their value can fluctuate widely and often. Companies will hit rough spots and perform poorly. Worst case scenario, a company will go out of business and its stock becomes worthless.

Because there is more risk involved with stocks, there is also generally more reward.

Bonds, meanwhile, are less risky. With a bond you are not buying a share of a company. You are buying a share of its debt. Think of it as an IOU. If a company (or a government body) needs money, it can issue bonds. When you buy a bond, you are essentially giving them money and they are agreeing to pay you back at a fixed interest rate.

Each will play a different role in your portfolio over the course of your lifetime. Think of stocks as long-term growth vehicles and think of bonds as vehicles that generate steadier streams of income.

The younger you are, the more your portfolio should consist of stocks.

"You're working with a longer horizon and that mitigates risk," says Steven Schwartz, founder of Wealth Design Services, a financial advisory firm in Rochester, New York. "It's not just that you have more time to earn back any money that you might have lost when your stocks performed poorly. Risk decreases as time lengthens."

This basic Investing 101 nugget can seem like more than you may ever wanted to know about money, but it will play a critical role in how much long-term wealth you accumulate. "Over the course of your life, your asset allocation will be more important than your market-timing," notes Jeffrey Zures.

Having the right mix of investments in your 401(k) at an early age can help you maximize the amount of money you save and earn over the course of your lifetime. Everyone has different comfort levels, but you don't want to be so conservative early on that you reduce your lifelong compounding power.

Most of the financial advisors I interviewed recommend that if you're in your 20s, you should have between 80 percent–90 percent of your 401(k) money invested in stocks, with the rest in bonds. (Some even argue that you could have 100 percent of your retirement savings invested in stocks.)

Over time, you will want to gradually reduce the amount of risk in your portfolio, which means you will decrease your allocations to stock and increase your investments in bonds.

By the time you retire, your asset allocation could be almost completely reversed from your younger years—perhaps using a portfolio that is 80 percent bonds and 20 percent stocks. At this point in your life, when you are retired, you will need your investments to generate income, not long-term growth.

This requires diligence and some work along the way. You need to make adjustments over time to tweak your overall asset allocation, but you also have to do some "rebalancing" as well. This just means that when certain parts of your portfolio perform better than others, you restore order.

So, if you're looking to maintain a mix of 80 percent stocks and 20 percent bonds mix, you will need to rebalance if one outperforms the other. If the stock market has a good year, your stocks will be worth more and your asset mix will change by itself. Your 80/20 portfolio may now be 85/15. You will want to sell off some of your funds that invest in stocks and buy more bond exposure to "rebalance."

You don't do this every day, but most advisors suggest you review and rebalance in your 401(k) once each year.

If this sounds like a tough task—picking the right funds out of the gate and then properly monitoring and tweaking your asset allocation on a regular basis—you're right. Very few people pick the right funds, and even fewer people ever bother to rebalance.[3]

You are not alone if this sounds like too much of a commitment to you. For a lot of people, they don't want to spend their time watching their 401(k) and worrying about whether or not they are properly allocated. It's not an easy job.

But it doesn't necessarily have to be that difficult either.

There are two relatively new options in the retirement world that can take care of all of this work on your behalf. If you're not inclined to actively manage your work-sponsored retirement plans, then help has arrived.

You just have to decide: Do you want help? Or do you want someone else to take care of it for you?

Life-Cycle Funds

If you want some help to get out of the gate properly with your 401(k), lifecycle funds can be a very good option for you to jump-start your account and set you on the right track in your formative saving years.

"A few years ago I came to realize that these types of lifecycle funds make a good deal of sense and could be the future of the 401(k)," says Ted Benna, president of the 401(k) Association, chief operating officer of Malvern Benefits Corp., and one of the pioneers who helped to develop and popularize 401(k) plans more than 20 years ago. "I've lived through the evolution of 401(k)s and seen where all the education has gotten plan participants over the years. There is no way to educate people enough. It's too difficult to move the bar. . . . Five years from now, I could see the vast majority of 401(k) assets being in lifecycle funds."

These lifecycle funds have been available to the general investing public since the 1990s, but they have started to gain serious traction in recent years. Part of the reason that they have grown in popularity is that more employers are now offering lifecycle funds as an option in 401(k) plans. And, as new legislation has motivated employers to automatically enroll people in 401(k)s, these same laws have also encouraged employers to make these types of automatic investments the default 401(k) option of choice.[4]

Simply put, lifecycle funds are essentially "all-in-one" mutual funds that that automatically invest and rebalance your holdings for you. Some lifecycle funds are target-date funds, which gradually rebalance and adjust your asset allocation based on the year that you think you will retire. These are also known as target-maturity funds. Other lifecycle funds are based on your age and your risk profile, so you choose a fund that is either aggressive, moderate or conservative and it too changes as you age and approach retirement.

Both are designed to be easy ways to "set-it-and-forget-it", if you will.

Sometimes lifecycle funds can be called lifestyle, target-date, target-maturity, balanced, or asset allocation funds, so just keep that in mind as you review the options in your 401(k) plan.

One of these funds is likely now on your 401(k) menu. Lifecycle funds are in roughly twice as many 401(k)s now as they were just a few years ago—roughly 66 percent of all 401(k) plans now have at least one lifecycle option to choose from.[5]

Most people I talk to point to the target-date funds as the most appropriate for a younger investor largely because all you have to do is select a fund based on the date you think you will retire. You don't have to think about your risk profile at all.

Ultimately, look for a fund that lists years next to its name and choose the one that is closest to the year that you think you will realistically stop working. For example, I use the "Destination 2045" fund.

Once you have selected a lifecycle fund based on your approximate retirement date, the fund will rebalance and gradually adjust your asset allocation for you over the years until you approach your target retirement. You will start out in your younger years with more investments in stocks than bonds and you will end up, at retirement age, with a more conservative and less risky investment mix. You don't have to rebalance every year and you don't have to think about the best ways to adjust your asset mix over time. You don't have to think about anything, really, if you don't want to.

You can ride a lifecycle fund out until you retire if you like, but you will always have the option of moving your money into other types of funds later in life as well. You're not locked into a lifecycle fund forever, it's your money.

"When you're 40 years old and you have more than $50,000 in your 401(k), then we can have a conversation about choosing the most optimal investment strategy for your portfolio if you like," says Steve Utkus, director of the Vanguard Center for Retirement Research. "But early on, your focus should be on saving; there is no need to over-focus on investing, especially with the one-stop-shop options that are now available in most retirement plans."

If it sounds simple, it's because that is exactly the idea behind lifecycle funds. Basically, these funds are just a collection of other mutual funds that have already been available on the market (and may even already be available in your 401(k) plan).

Some of the mutual funds in a lifecycle fund will invest in different types of stocks (either directly in individual stocks or in mutual funds), while others will invest in bonds or even real estate. Different fund companies will take different approaches to lifecycle funds. Conceptually, however, they all have the same function: grow your money early on and preserve it for later in life.

When using any kind of lifecycle fund, you are essentially picking one fund that contains all of the individual funds you would need to properly build a balanced portfolio. All of the education and advice in the world can really only help you to create, from the funds available in your 401(k), what ultimately would amount to the same thing as a lifecycle fund at the end of the day.

It's not just that these funds are investing in stocks and bonds based on something like your age or risk appetite. There are other levels of investment diversification in play here. Let's just say your lifecycle fund starts you out by putting 80 percent of your 401(k) money in mutual funds that invest in stocks. Within this portion of your 401(k) portfolio, a lifecycle fund could divide up your investments into U.S. stocks, international stocks—or even emerging markets stocks that include stocks from countries with less-developed stock markets such as China, India, Taiwan, Brazil, or Russia.

The idea here again is to lower your overall risk through diversification. If the U.S. markets struggle, for example, this layer of diversification provides you with some additional protection from underperformance. If emerging markets have a great year, you don't miss out, and you may be able to use this outperformance to make up for other areas of underperformance. Also, keeping with the same example, if emerging markets have a great year, the lifecycle fund will sell off some of the gains you have made in this market to make sure your investments stay balanced, and you are not totally "overweight" or "underweight" in any one part of your asset allocation.

This is another important feature of a lifecycle fund. Because of this automatic rebalancing, studies have shown that people who use lifecycle funds in their 401(k) have received better overall investment returns than those people who actively rebalanced their 401(k)s on their own. One study, which was issued by the Pension Research Council in 2006, found that participants in balanced or lifecycle funds that leave trading and rebalancing to a fund's portfolio manager earned excess returns of 84 basis points on a risk adjusted basis (84 basis points=0.84%).[6] Those who actively rebalanced on their own, in comparison, earned only 26 basis points on a risk-adjusted basis.

It may not sound like a big deal, but if you could improve your investment returns by more than half of a percent, wouldn't you? It's hard to say no, especially if you had to do less to earn more.

Every lifecycle fund will take a different approach to investing your money. Some may start you out with 90 percent equity exposure and 10 percent bonds, while another fund could be an 80 percent stock and 20 percent bond mix, and yet another could start you out at a 70 percent/30 percent mix.

Some may invest your money in index funds—these are passive investments that aim to get you the same returns as the markets. Others may take an active approach, which means that they are actively trading to try and beat the markets. This will play a major role in the investment management fees that you will pay for a lifecycle fund. The more active investment management that goes into the lifecycle fund, the more you will pay in fees.

These expense ratios—the percentage of assets managed that a company charges to cover their overhead—vary widely. They really depend on the fund's style of management as well as the particular fund company that is managing the fund. Some companies are just more expensive than others; but ultimately, in a 401(k) you have to choose a fund from the menu of funds being made available to you by your employer.

If your employer is presenting you with more than one type of lifecycle fund to use in your 401(k), consider the expenses of each carefully. Because you are going to make a lifecycle fund the sole focus of your 401(k) for now, try and choose the fund that has the lowest fees (even if the other funds have shown a history of stronger past performance). Again, in the long run, what you pay in fees will have an impact on what you earn from your investments. Think of fees as negative investment performance. The larger the fee, the better a fund has to do to get you your money back; and even if a fund doesn't produce great results, you still have to pay the fee.

No matter what the actual investment philosophy and strategy is behind the lifecycle fund that may be offered in your 401(k) plan, the core concept will always be the same: build your money up at first with some more aggressive investing, then turn the risk down a notch as you age. You opt in and the pros will take care of the rest.

Steve Utkus also notes one more very important thing about lifecycle/target-date funds: Most people actually use them improperly. These types of funds are designed to take on *all* of your 401(k) money. Yet only about one-third of 401(k) participants who use lifecycle funds, actually use one lifecycle fund. This is the proper way to use a lifecycle fund.

Most people who select a lifecycle fund unfortunately also select several other funds that are available in their 401(k) thinking that this may be creating a more diverse portfolio.

Lifecycle funds are designed to cover your all of your 401(k) diversification from soup to nuts. Investing in other types of funds in addition to a lifecycle fund only defeats this purpose. You wouldn't pay for an all-you-can-eat buffet and start ordering all types of other foods directly from the menu. Take the same approach here.

Ironically, with lifecycle funds you get the maximum benefits of diversification by being invested in just one fund. Just think of this one fund as a collection, or a basket, of other funds. Yet this is one basket where you can, and should, put all of your eggs.

Managed Accounts

With a lifecycle fund, you are making the decision to choose one fund that will help you invest your 401(k) money properly for the rest of your life. If picking just one fund sounds like it may be too much, and you want to completely check yourself out of managing your 401(k), help has arrived.

More employers are now starting to offer managed account programs, or managed 401(k)s, as part of their retirement plans.[7] Almost one in 10 employers now offers such and option, according to Hewitt Associates.[8]

In some cases, just as with lifecycle funds, managed accounts are being used as the default investment option for new employees if they are automatically enrolled in a 401(k). So, even if it is not an option for you right now, there is a pretty good chance that you will run into managed accounts at your next job.

A managed account program does not require you to pick any of the fund options in your 401(k). In fact, you don't even have to look at the funds if you don't want to—you can just check off of the box among your retirement plan options that says "managed accounts" or "managed 401(k)" and you won't have to make any further investment decisions if you don't want to.

Think of a managed account as basically being a shortcut to a financial advisor who doesn't just provide you with advice—they will actually manage your 401(k) portfolio for you.

But they don't just run your 401(k) with an eye on factors such as your age or your risk tolerance. In a managed 401(k), you get a customized 401(k) portfolio designed to complement any existing investments that you may have outside of your 401(k), including any other kinds of retirement savings vehicles, like an IRA. They'll even consider the investments that your spouse may have if you're married, for instance. It also will allow you to have some level of company stock in your 401(k), if you work for a publicly traded company, something you may miss out on with a lifecycle fund.

Your age, desired retirement date, and risk tolerance are factored in as well; but a more thorough evaluation process allows your employer's managed account provider to devise a more comprehensive portfolio based on your total picture—not just your timeline.

The more information you are willing to disclose, the more a managed account program can be tailored to your specific profile. And that's the primary difference between a managed account and a lifecycle fund. While you can set it and forget it with a lifecycle fund and it ages with you, it doesn't change as your life changes. It's a one-size-fits-all approach that can be effective in helping you have a proper retirement savings—after all, you're buying into a prudently managed fund that will rebalance for you and tweak your mix of investments. It's also the same fund that many other people who are close to you in age are buying as well.

According to Don Salama, senior managing director and head of retirement plan services at New York Life Investment Management, managed accounts ultimately consider all of your specific variables. And the younger you are, the more changes you will encounter throughout the rest of your working life. "If you start out in a managed account program and then you get married a few years later, or buy a house, or have child, the managed account will adjust your 401(k) portfolio accordingly," he says.

It's not just about avoiding common 401(k) mistakes and picking the right funds; the managed account is an attempt to build a retirement savings vehicle that properly and continuously sums up of all your parts.

The idea is really to recognize that two people who are the exact same age may have completely different lives and investment needs. Just consider the tremendous differences in income levels among younger workers. I have interviewed dozens of people in their early 20s and their incomes have ranged from $25,000 a year all the way up to almost $100,000 a year. When you earn more, you can do more with your money. Their *total* portfolio should look different than someone who is trying to slowly build enough savings to have a portfolio.

The 25-year-old earning close to six figures may, for example, have a brokerage account or may own some mutual funds that they purchased directly outside of the retirement plan. They may also own a home. The managed account would choose funds and construct an asset allocation for his or her 401(k) that would take these other investments into account. If, for example, he or she is heavily invested in technology stocks outside of the 401(k), the managed account provider would likely look to invest the 401(k) money in other sectors of the stock market. Again, one of the keys to building long-term wealth is diversification, so it's important that your money is never too concentrated in any one area. Managed accounts will take care of the diversification for you and do so in the scheme of your total portfolio (not to mention what your spouse may have in his or her portfolio as well).

Because managed accounts are more involved than other automatic options such as the lifecycle fund, they also tend to be more expensive options too. Again the fees vary depending on who is providing the managed account services to your employer. Generally, you pay a fee for the managed account service and then another level of investment management fees for any of the funds that the managed account provider invests your money in. While you get more with the managed account, you also pay an additional layer of fees for the advisory services.

The managed account fees vary depending on how much money you have in your 401(k). If you have under $50,000, for instance, you often pay a higher rate than someone who has more than $250,000. The less you have, the more you may pay, relatively speaking.

In a typical managed account program, the fees could range from 10 to 75 basis points, according to a survey from Hewitt Associates, on top of the fees you will pay for the underlying funds.[9] So, for someone who has a balance of $25,000 in their 401(k) with a fee of 50 basis points, they will pay $125 that year for a managed account, plus the standard investment fees on the funds their money is invested in.

It's also important to note that while there is an extra layer of fees with managed accounts, it is extended to you at a price well-below market value. Because the service is delivered through your employer, they have hopefully negotiated for an institutional discount. On your own, you could pay as much as four or five times the price for these kinds of investment services.

You are paying for investment advice and implementation that *could* help your 401(k) perform better than something less customized, such as a lifecycle fund. So the extra fees could pay for themselves and then some. But this is *not* a guarantee. Ultimately, you are paying for the chance to outperform, not the certainty of outperformance.

It's important again to note the fees and how they work against investment performance. Paying 30 basis points more in annual fees every year until you retire could lower your final 401(k) balance by almost 10 percent, according to Hewitt.

If your managed account option is significantly more expensive than the lifecycle option in your plan, consider how much money is in your 401(k) and think about how many life changes you realistically expect to encounter over the next few years. Consider how much you really need—and stand to benefit—from paying more for more comprehensive investment management services.

You could always jumpstart your 401(k) by beginning in a lifecycle fund and then eventually graduate to a managed account program as time goes on. The more time passes, the more money you will likely have inside and outside of your 401(k). And as your 401k balance increases, your managed account fees will decline as well.

Remember, you're young and trying to accumulate assets should be your top priority early on. So consider that you are taking a chance when you elect to pay higher fees for more account management. It might pay off, it might not, or it could be a wash. You make the decision and you have to be comfortable with the choices you make. Ultimately, it's like any other purchase we make every day. Some people always choose to fill up their cars with super-ultra-premium gasoline, while others opt for regular. In the end, it comes down to how much you care about your expenses, or how much you value performance.

———————————

If both managed accounts and lifecycle funds are made available to you through your 401(k), don't stress out over making a decision. For most of us, both are better options than doing it yourself for the next 30 or 40 years.

Think of managed accounts as "advanced autopilot"; and the more you have, the more sense a managed 401(k) may be for you. If you're just starting out and building your 401(k) from scratch you shouldn't completely dismiss managed accounts because your earnings, savings, and life could change dramatically over the next five to 10 years.

If you are starting a new job and you are going to participate in a retirement plan, look for these automatic investment options.

If you are already contributing to a work-sponsored retirement plan and you're not sure how your money is invested, *find out.*

If you don't understand, *ask somebody.*

You don't have to wait until you start another job to put yourself on autopilot. You can do it right now. Ask your human resources people or your retirement plan administrators if you have a lifecycle or managed account option. If your money was defaulted into a weak stable-value or money market fund, then move it immediately. Again, if you don't know, *find out.*

If you've allocated yourself across a handful of funds that you picked out yourself, still consider either option because it will mean you will have to do less maintenance over the years to make sure everything is in order.

By participating, you have already taken the most important step. These newer options like managed accounts and lifecycle funds are just there to make sure that you are on the right track—and that you stay there until you are ready to retire.

You don't need to be intimidated or distracted anymore. You don't need to be over-involved if you don't want to.

You just need to plug in and turn on.

Sound simple enough?

That's the point.

CHAPTER 10

The Teacher with More to Learn

Marisa, 26, hoards money. Even as a little kid, when her father would give her and her sisters quarters to go play arcade games on family vacations, she'd put the money in her luggage and bring it home to the shoebox under her bed.

She was satisfied with watching everyone else play games and claimed that she didn't want to play because she didn't "enjoy competition."

But the truth is she always knew that someday she would want that money more—much more than she felt the need to play Ms. Pac-Man at that very moment.

Video games every weekend? She'd rather buy herself a decent piece of jewelry every couple of years. That's if she could tolerate the thought of spending. Most of her money would eventually end up in her shoebox under her bed.

Now she still hoards money, but she's uploaded her old school savings tactics to her 26-year-old life.

She has never *once* in her life carried a credit card balance. She has never once been in debt. Somehow, she says, she pulled this off when she was living a six-figure lifestyle in a New York City doorman building on just a $30,000 yearly salary.

Marisa has continuously put what money she could into traditional savings accounts and CDs since she graduated college nine years ago, but that's it. She's never really graduated from the shoe box savings strategies of a little kid.

She has thought about buying a house, and she's thought about how expensive it might be to have a child one day. She's never thought about retirement, much less saving for it, even though she's had several golden opportunities.

She had five jobs in her first five years out of school, mostly corporate PR gigs that make *The Devil Wears Prada* look like *Bambi*. After years of thankless days and nights, she gave it up to become a teacher. She had enough of PR. She wanted more out of life.

The novelty of rubbing elbows with Lenny Kravitz or Naomi Campbell at a cocktail party or red carpet event wore off seamlessly. She became disenchanted with her career almost as quickly as she moved from one New York PR shop to another.

Marisa could tell you the name of every celebrity she ever worked with, or every coworker she closed out a bar with on a work night.

Remarkably, she has no idea if any of her previous five employers offered her any kind of retirement plan.

She may have contributed to some of these plans, she admits, even if she wasn't sure if they existed or not.

One day last year she got a statement from one of her former employers about "some kind of retirement fund." She's not sure what it was and why she had any money in this account. "People told me that the company had great benefits," she says. "I guess they were right."

On her own, she contributed $1,000 to an IRA a couple of times right before she filed her taxes. Her accountant told her it would allow her to save for her future; but it would also help her collect a larger tax refund for the year.

It did. She took that refund straight to the bank. And put it directly into her savings account, of course.

Now she's married and teaching full-time. She's saved more than $30,000 of her own money, none of it working very hard in her bank accounts. She also has another $15,000 in a joint savings account with her husband not doing much more than sitting still at "maybe" a 1.5 percent rate, she says.

Marisa is still debt-free, dreams of having children and owning an apartment. She's a teacher now, and she's been satisfied with this career so far.

She makes decent money teaching, about $55,000 a year, and tutors on the side for extra cash.

As a teacher and a New York City employee, she has one of the best retirement setups going. The Board of Education automatically enrolled her in the city teachers' retirement system, which is a good thing because she had no idea that she was eligible. She has no idea how much she may have accumulated over the past school year, but she says she's also okay with not knowing.

She is also able to put money in a tax-deferred annuity through her teachers' union that guarantees an annual return of at least 7 percent. She hasn't set this up yet; but she admits she probably shouldn't wait. She knows she should do it, but she's also not exactly sure what it is. Marisa also hasn't contributed to her traditional IRA in four years and she knows she should probably put some money here as well.

She is still putting money into savings every month, saving for a rainy day, saving for an apartment with her husband, and saving for a baby that they'd like to have in the next few years, although they're in no rush.

Now Marisa is starting to realize that she should be saving more efficiently, and she is also starting to think a little bit more about her retirement—mostly because she sees her parents taking inventory of their own financials to figure out when they should stop working.

Part of Marisa had always thought that her husband would support them both during retirement. Now she has a better understanding of the cost of living.

Last week, she says she fell in love with a one-bedroom apartment in New York that was selling for $550,000. She admits it sounded like a great deal, but she also admits that her perspective is jaded. She realizes that even after they pony up more than $100,000 for the down payment, they're still on the hook for a more than $400,000 mortgage.

She can't understand how they will cover that and have a baby in the next couple of years; she can't even fathom how they will pay for their retirement.

"It just seems like there's too much coming up too soon," she says. "I'll need every dollar. For something."

Now, mostly out of fear, she's saving a bit more each month.

The bad news is she's not using her money as wisely or as effectively as she could.

The good news? Marisa's still hoarding.

Prescription

Marisa understands, perhaps better than most people, the need to live within her means and save for the things in life that are most important to her, according to Bruce Primeau, vice president of wealth management services at Wade Financial Group in Minneapolis.

While she's wired to save, Primeau also thinks it should not come at the expense of living her life to the fullest. Fear can be a great motivator in many cases; but Marisa's first move should be to put together a real financial game plan. Right now she saves without a real purpose. Outlining a financial game plan allows her to get her arms around how effectively she is saving for both her short-term and long-term financial needs, which might help her feel more confident that she is moving in the right direction.

She's lucky that she's automatically covered in one retirement plan through the Board of Education—but she still needs to be careful not to rely on this as her sole source of retirement savings. Her husband certainly won't be able to support them both during their retirement if they want to maintain a decent standard of living.

Because Marisa also has the opportunity to save money on a pretax, tax-deferred basis through her union, Primeau thinks she should figure out what portion of her income she could commit to this separate retirement plan. Rather than saving in a traditional bank account, she should now consider placing her money into this supplemental retirement account moving forward. Given her income, she would likely save an additional 30 to 40 cents on the dollar by saving in a pretax retirement account, instead of putting after-tax dollars into a savings account.

Overall Marisa should be aiming to put roughly 10 percent of her gross pay towards retirement, with 5 percent or 6 percent going into this tax-deferred annuity. Because she is young, she should invest this money "somewhat aggressively," says Primeau, with 60 percent to 80 percent of the money in equities (stocks). He estimates that a balanced portfolio of 60 percent to 80 percent equities and 20 percent to 40 percent bonds, over time, should return between 9 percent and 11 percent.

Aside from this employer-sponsored account, Marisa should also seriously consider opening up a Roth IRA. If she's putting 6 percent of her gross pay, or $3,300, towards her tax-deferred annuity, then she should put 4 percent, or $2,200, towards a Roth IRA, for a total of $5,500 in retirement savings each year. The Roth is funded with after-tax dollars, but she won't be taxed when she takes the money out after she turns 59.5 years old. Having a balance of both types of accounts is what Primeau thinks would be best for Marisa when she is retired.

As for the money that Marisa has already saved, this should be used for the down payment on the purchase of her first home. For her home purchase, Primeau suggests that Marisa and her husband would likely want to shoot for a 20 percent down payment to avoid paying mortgage insurance. They should also look to pay off the loan over a 30-year period at a roughly 6.5 percent pretax rate.

At the moment, Marisa should move any money that she has already saved in CDs into a money market account as soon as the CD matures. She may need this money any day now for her home and she does not want to have it locked up. She'll be penalized if she has to withdraw it early.

And this should really be the last time that Marisa considers using CDs or traditional bank accounts as the primary source for her savings. Her inclination to hoard is great; she just needs a little guidance to make it grow properly. "She should invest her savings more appropriately according to their purpose throughout the rest of her life," says Primeau, adding that her savings should be divided up into different baskets, such as retirement, home down payment, and her future children's college.

While she's saving her money, she has essentially been saving blindly. Her worst case scenario won't be that bad if she keeps up her current behavior, but her best-case-scenario could certainly be a lot better.

In your younger years, savings accounts and CDs are not good long-term answers for life expenses according to Primeau. While rates on these types of investments are at 4 percent or 5 percent now, it wasn't that long ago that savings accounts were paying less than 1 percent interest while CDs were in the 3 percent neighborhood. These are, to Primeau, decent vehicles for emergency funds or if you need some short-term liquidity, but not for longer-term expenses.

This is especially important for Marisa to recognize now, because she's about to buy her first home. Not only will her life expenses likely increase, but the money she puts into her house every month is essentially "dead dollars," says Primeau. She won't earn any interest or receive dividend pay outs while she's putting money into her mortgage. With a home, essentially, the return on your principal investment is zero. (It's only worth something when you sell it.)

While a home holds the promise of being a great long-term investment, Marisa should start to learn more about what she can do with her money in the short term. She can't rely on people to always point her in the right direction.

She should put her retirement contributions on autopilot. Then she should start educating herself about other types of investments, including mutual funds and exchange-traded funds, which are readily available and easy to understand. Even if they sound like foreign concepts to her now, Marisa's financial understanding should mature at the same rate as everything else in her life.

"Ignorance is no excuse for not knowing how to take advantage of opportunities as they become available," Bruce Primeau says. "It's never too early, or too late to become educated."

CHAPTER

11

Dealing with Debt and Fighting Gravity

When I hear someone start a sentence with "The problem with our generation," I go deaf.

Intentionally.

One of my good friends, however, caught my ear during a weak moment. I'm glad he did.

"The problem with our generation," he began, "is that we never see money. Money has always been just a concept. It's not real. It only *is* because we say it *is*."

Now, without much visibility, money has become an even more far-fetched concept to many.

There is no real payday sensation anymore. Instead of getting a fistful of cash for your labor, now direct deposits just move the numbers in your bank account every couple of weeks.

Cash has taken a back seat to credit cards and debit cards.

Bills are easily paid online or over the phone.

Cash is a last resort.

We understand what cash is literally worth, but we have little concept for its actual value. Money has, in many cases, become an allowance, rather than a source of income.

Yet we still find ways to live beyond our allowances—and it seems that we're doing this more and more every year.

The average revolving debt for someone in their 20s has now hit $5,781 according to credit agency Experian, which polled more than

3 million 20-somethings. This debt, which includes credit card debt, is up by almost 25 percent from five years ago.[1]

This should come as little surprise. People are increasingly getting into debt *before* they even really start earning money. Almost 85 percent of college students have at least one credit card, with the average balance hovering at more than $2,300.[2]

While the debt levels in theory may seem manageable, where do we go from here?

Life is expensive, sure, and it may be impossible to avoid taking on certain types of "good debt," including student loans and mortgages. With these debts, at least you are getting *something* in return, and at least it is a step towards personal advancement.

It's the consumer debt that is most troubling; it's quicksand. You get nothing in return except more debt if you can't pay the initial debt off quickly enough. It not only prevents you from putting money away now, it also subtracts from your ability have more money in the future.

"Credit does not exist for you to fulfill your every wish," says Cheryl Hancock, financial planner at Rinehart & Associates in Charlotte, North Carolina. "There are bad consequences when you abuse this privilege. Too many young workers seem to think that they have to have it *all* right now and therefore go to extremes to get it. You have to be forward thinking at all times. How does this action I'm contemplating today affect me down the road?"

As the debt mounts, it attacks our ability to think long-term. How can you think about saving for a house—let alone retirement—when you're staring at a credit card balance that just never seems to move in the right direction?

The truth is you can, because you have no choice. It's comes down to getting squeezed now or getting squeezed later.

Just because you carry a debt does not mean that you should be completely ignoring your retirement. Getting out of debt is one of the most important things you can do to improve you financial health—some would argue it's the most important.

Depending on the type and the amount of debt that you may be carrying, there are different approaches that you may want to take to balance your immediate debts with your need to save for the long-term.

Otherwise, in 30 or 40 years, there may be a whole new problem with our generation.

Fighting Gravity

Here's another grim reality: Only a lucky minority of people are now graduating from college without owing somebody money for something.

The economics involved just weren't going to work out in our favor. The average cost of college has increased at roughly twice the rate of inflation in recent years, so student loans have been the only recourse for many people seeking higher education.

More than half of recent college graduates now have some level of student loans outstanding, according to the National Center for Education Statistics.[3] Most college students take out an average of almost $20,000 in student loans now, and graduate with an average outstanding balance of roughly $10,000.

So before many people even get to the point where they can start earning money, they're already in the hole for thousands of dollars. And that's just for a bachelor's degree.

Higher education costs ultimately help you increase your knowledge base and your earning potential, one of the reasons that student loans can be categorized as "good debt." Education will always be a valuable commodity, no matter the expense.

But good or bad debt, it's still debt. It's a drag on your earnings and your saving potential because not only did you borrow money, you must pay it back with interest.

"By carrying any kind of debt, you are agreeing to a negative investment return," says Sid Blum, financial planner and founder of GreenLight Advisors in Evanston, Illinois. "That's all an interest rate is, most people just don't take the time to think about it."

Blum points out that with student loans, the interest you pay can be tax deductible—up to $2,500 in 2007—which helps to lessen its negative investment return.

Blum, however, and many other financial advisors say that refinancing your loans should be one of the first things you look to do. You may be able to lower your interest rates, which help lower your monthly payments and reduce your long-term debt.

Generally, interest rates on student loans should be relatively low (especially compared with credit card rates), but the lower you can get your rate, the better. According to Diane Pearson, director of financial planning and a wealth advisor at Legend Financial Advisors in Pittsburgh, "You need to explore every possible method to get these rates down. Some lenders, if you agree to pay your student loans back online, for instance, might even drop your rates a little bit lower." She adds, "Every little bit helps, so exhaust every option to reduce your total payments."

Pearson recommends that with student loans it may help to extend the duration of the loan, provided that your interest rates are not prohibitive. "There's no need to rush," she says. "If you can pay the loan back in 10 years instead of five and lower your monthly payments, it will help you free up some extra cash in your early working years."

To Pearson, this is money that should not be spent freely. It should be dedicated to other needs, including setting up an emergency fund (maybe four months of living expenses) and making contributions to a work-sponsored retirement plan.

If you're eligible for any level of match in a work-sponsored retirement plan, advisors suggest that you should take advantage of the opportunity to take the free money—even if you're still paying off any debts. And, if possible, contribute enough to get the full match.

"You will never be able to recapture those years," says Morgan Stone, a certified financial planner at Stone Asset Management in Austin, Texas. "If you have $30,000 in credit card debt at a young age, which is extreme, then paying that down should be your top priority, otherwise it will follow you around forever. But if you have student loans outstanding or a relatively small credit card balance, then you can budget for savings."

If you are getting a match and if your debt is manageable, then you should budget to pay off your balance and contribute to a work-sponsored plan at the same time, even if your contribution is only in the neighborhood of $50 to $100 each month, says Blum. Again, he says to view interest rates and matching rates as investment returns. If your employer will match $0.50 for every dollar you contribute, that is a 50 percent return on your investment. Even if your credit card rate is high, say 25 percent, a contribution to a 401(k) plan that matches every dollar is a significantly better investment, Blum says.

Also, let's be honest. Forget the financial advisors for a second— let's just say you pass on making contributions to your 401(k) because you think you should be solely focused on your credit card debt. Fine. Fair enough. But where's that would-be 401(k) money going to go? Are you going to put it towards paying off your credit card debt, or are you going to spend it? You need to ask yourself these questions because only you know your tendencies and limitations. Remember, your 401(k) contributions are *automatically* deducted from your *gross* pay. This is a good way to police yourself. And not only will your savings be on autopilot, but consider the math at work here too. Let's say you contribute $50 each month to your 401(k) and you're getting a dollar-for dollar match from your employer. That's a true, pretax $50, plus another $50 for free from your employer.

Or you could opt to keep that $50 each month. It will come out of your net pay, so figure it's worth about $38 after taxes.

You're looking at a real $100 saved every month, or potentially $38 spent. You could plow through that in a night out. You could burn through it in an hour without trying.

The decision is yours to make. You could put away $1,200 in a year that will compound for 30 or 40 years, or you could choose to have another $456 in your pocket. Until you spend it.

Credit card debt is a killer. It is the most hazardous threat to your young financial well-being.

With any kind of consumer credit card debt, it's even more critical to get your interest rates lowered. For one, unlike student loan interest, credit card interest is *not* tax-deductible.

Also, because the interest rates on credit cards can be so high— the average consumer credit card interest rate is roughly 15 percent[4]—it can be really damaging to both your short and long-term saving capacity.

There are a lot of different ways that you can go about attempting to lower the rates on your credit cards.

The easiest way can be to call your credit card company and just ask. I know, it sounds ridiculous, but it really can be that easy. There is so much competition in the credit card industry that you can actually turn this around and use it to your advantage.

There's no science here, you just need to do it. If you don't ask, the answer is always no.

If, for some reason they say no at first, tell them that you can get a better rate on another card and you will just transfer your balance if they can't help you out. Or just call back and ask again, you might get a different person who's more willing to come through for you.

And just to give you an idea how easy it may be to lower you rate just by picking up the phone, consider a recent study from the U.S. Public Interest Research Group in Washington D.C. They had 50 different people from across the United States call their creditors and ask for lower rates, More than half—28 of the 50 participants—were able to get a lower rate with a single phone call.[5]

Some even managed to get their interest rate dropped to 0 percent temporarily. Roughly 10 minutes of work on the phone could help you save hundreds or thousands of dollars that you would have owed to a credit card company. So, if you haven't done this already, do it. And if you have, do it again. What's the worst that can happen?

Another option is to do a balance transfer to a card that charges a lower interest rate. And if you have multiple credit card debts, you may even want to consider consolidating them all together on a single card that will give you the lowest rate possible.

Again, because of the competition in the credit card industry, there are a lot of opportunities for you to transfer your debt to cards that temporarily won't charge you any interest at all. Typically, you can get about six to 12 months at 0 percent before a rate—usually a hefty one—will kick in.

As Diane Pearson says, this can be a particularly good move if you can pay off your entire credit card balance in the amount of time that you won't be getting charged interest. Because the rates can be unusually high, however, once the "teaser" period is up, you want to make sure that you're not putting yourself in situation that can be worse down the road.

Do the math. There's no interest to figure out, so just divide up your balance by the number of 0 percent months and figure out if this is doable.

You do need to be very careful. Read all of the fine print with these transfer transactions. Some cards only charge you 0 percent interest on the balance you transfer over—but any new purchases made on the card may involve a separate interest rate. If this is the case, don't carry the card in your wallet. Consider it as nothing more than a loan that has to be paid off during a specific period of time.

Also make sure you find out if there are any fees involved to do the transfer. If there are, shop around, you shouldn't pay for the right to pay someone else your debt.

Once you have lowered your interest rates, planners suggest you do a budget and figure out a way to pay above the monthly minimums due each month. Shoot for at least twice the minimum, if possible, otherwise the tag-team combo of interest and minimum payments can make the power of compounding work against you in a big way.

Consider these long-term effects: If you have a credit card balance of $5,000 and your annual interest rate is 20 percent, it will take you almost 21 years and cost you $5,991 in total interest to erase that debt if you strictly write a check for a minimum payment of 3 percent each month.

But what if you were able to cut your interest rate in half? If you could negotiate your interest rate down to 10 percent, then it will lower the amount of total interest you pay by almost $4,200 and you will have paid off your balance in just under 14 years.

That's a huge difference in the long run and it didn't require much more than a little effort to lower your rate.

If you really want to make a dent in your debt, you will have to find a way to make more than the minimum monthly payments. This can be even more powerful than lowering your interest rate.

Let's keep with the same scenario from above. Now you've lowered your interest rate to 10 percent, and, instead of paying 3 percent of what you owe every month you commit to paying off 6 percent of your balance.

By paying $300 each month instead of $150, you can erase your $5,000 balance in 19 months instead of 14 years. You will also end up paying $405 in total interest, instead of roughly $1,800.

The power of compounding works both ways.

––––––––––––

If you are not comfortable contributing to a work-sponsored retirement plan because you are committed to erasing your debt as quickly as possible, that's fine. We all have different comfort levels and preferences.

But if you have budgeted well enough to pay down your debts, you might want to carry your diligence over to your retirement savings for a little while to try and make up for lost time.

Keep with your savings plan. Say you've been setting aside $300 a month for your credit card. Think about putting this same amount in your 401(k) for a year, even if it's above the level your employer is willing to match.

If you earn $30,000 a year and your employer will match your contributions up to 6 percent of your salary, make the 6 percent contribution first and foremost. This comes out to $1,800 during the year, or $150 per month.

Now, given that you learned to live without $300 a month when you were making your credit card payments, give some thought about putting this same amount into your 401(k) for a year. After all, living on this budget allowed you to lead a manageable lifestyle. Remember, its pretax dollars again that go into your 401(k). So, because this $300 doesn't come out of your net take-home pay, you're already guaranteed a bit more breathing room by dedicating the same dollar amount to your 401(k) that you were to your credit card. (Hopefully, you're earning more money as well.)

Also keep in mind that you can contribute up to $15,500 each year to your 401(k). So you can play a little catch up if you're ever stunted by debts early on. It's just important to recognize that you need to manage the money that you owe as much as the money that you have saved. Debt and saving are siblings—and you are in a position to mediate any rivalries. We work unbelievably hard to earn more money; yet it's amazing how few people will put in any effort to easily lower their credit card rates. The two sides of the ledger go hand-in-hand, and they will forever.

CHAPTER 12

The Mayor's Lounge

Orin can't sit still.

Maybe it's because he's a numbers guy, but at the age of 32, he's packed in more living than most people could ever handle in a lifetime.

"I'm not going to live forever," he says. "I want to get it all in while I can. I probably haven't said 'no' too many times in my life.

But I don't regret a single time I've ever said yes."

He's driven to or through practically every state in the United States. Name a foreign country and there's a good chance that he's been there. Name a beer and there's probably an even better chance that he drank it.

Orin doesn't stop, even when he is not physically on the move. He's always been playing at least two hands at once, always thinking about *now* with an eye on *later*.

When he was a high school student by day, he was a guitarist and a singer by night. He signed a record deal with a small label at 16, recorded an album before he turned 17, and had a song on the radio before he had a high school diploma.

In college, he was one part student, one part rock star and one part accountant at a local tax firm. (Music is his religion, he says. As a number's guy, however, he knows the odds of Plan A working out. For this reason, he understands the value of having a Plan B.)

While he graduated from college 10 years ago, he never left that lifestyle too far behind.

He's still everywhere, but now he just has his hands in a lot of grown up places. In a small town outside of Philly, where he's an accountant full-time, he's been organizing music festivals, playing in various clubs and bars, and he's somehow found the time to host a radio show on occasion.

If that wasn't enough, Orin started to turn himself into a mini-corporation on the side.

With some of his extra cash, he's bought and flipped some properties for a decent profit over the last few years. He's hung on to a couple of residential places, one where he now lives with his wife, and two other places where he's collecting rent from several tenants.

In his town, if Orin's not your friend, then you probably do business with him.

He knows everyone, and everyone knows Orin.

There's a reason his friends call him "The Mayor."

All of his moves are calculated, always with purpose and intent and rarely just out of restlessness. His mind's eye has been staring down one vision for years.

His goal: make as much money as possible with these real estate ventures and open up his own music club, the Mayor's Lounge.

He already has the space. He found an old warehouse in the center of town that was for sale about two years ago. He got the price down to $70,000 and took out a mortgage to finance the dream. It needed work, and lots of it, but for Orin it was just another project to push forward.

He figured he could finance the renovations with the income he was getting from his tenants, as well as some of the money he already earned from selling his first few properties.

And on paper, not surprisingly, he had it all figured out. The numbers were going to work out perfectly.

But then everything changed.

Everything.

His wife was pregnant.

There was a baby on the way.

In nine months, he knew his life would never be the same again.

He needed a change of plans, unless he could figure out a way to put a crib in a quiet place at the Mayor's Lounge.

Instead of pumping money into the club, his extra income went into his home. He renovated his house. He built a nursery and bought all the right furniture. He wanted everything to be perfect when the baby came, no questions asked. "My parents took good care of me," he says. "I've always known I wanted to do the same thing for my kids."

He tried to work on the club, but his focus wasn't completely there and nine months went by in a blink.

Now he's a father to a beautiful baby girl, right when he thought he'd be cutting the ribbon on his club. "Things are working out differently than I planned," he says. "But I'm lucky that at least they're working out."

His wife is only working part-time so she can spend more time at home with their daughter, which puts Orin on the hook to take care of almost all of their expenses. He started to put together a budget for the first time in his life because he realizes he has no choice. With a baby in his life, there's no such thing as "extra."

Before his daughter was born, most of his excess cash had gone into his real estate, his travel and his inability to say no over the years. He's always thought about retirement, enough to plug about 10 percent of his pay into his 401(k).

"I know I don't want to work until I die. Putting a little money away every month just sounds like a better option," he says, sounding as if he's never really questioned that he could take care of himself.

He does wonder if he should keep putting this much money into his 401(k). He had toyed with the idea of starting a Roth not long ago, but that's not in the cards right now.

Now he has to think about paying for more than just his own future. And while he can tell you how much he'll spend on diapers over the next 18 months, he can't even begin to estimate what it might cost to send his daughter to college in 18 years.

He hasn't started saving for her education yet, and he says his hands are tied until his wife goes back to work full-time.

He still has two apartments that he owns, which helps a little. The money he's making off of his tenants is going towards mortgage payments and is also taking care of bills at home that used to be covered by his wife's paychecks.

They're living just fine, by most standards, they're just living differently. They have three people living off of slightly more than one income when only a year ago they had two incomes to take care of two adults.

The Mayor's Lounge still needs heat, a new bathroom, and sprinklers before Orin can open the doors to the public. But he hasn't dismissed that it will still get done.

He knows it will all get done.

He's lived like this before.

He's lived like this forever, actually.

"If I stopped everything, I'd be somebody else," he says.

"Plans change. But people don't have to."

Prescription

There are some people who can have a savings plan delivered to them in a box.

Orin is not one of these people.

Because he started saving for his retirement several years ago, and because he already owns his home, Orin now has some flexibility to deal with the recent developments in his life, according to Timothy Maurer, director of financial planning at The Financial Consulate in Baltimore. "The real question is how to prioritize the incoming funds," he says.

Ultimately, Orin doesn't need to save *more* money right now; he just needs to keep saving the same amount in a slightly different capacity. So even though he thinks his wife has to go back to work before he can start saving for his daughter's college, he's mistaken.

Orin is already in the habit of contributing 10 percent of his pay to his work-sponsored retirement plan. Now he just needs to cut this back a bit and steer a chunk towards some other savings vehicles.

With his 401(k), Orin should only be contributing as much as he needs to get the full match from his employer. As Maurer suggests, if they match up to 6 percent, Orin should now only contribute 6 percent of his pay and then direct the other 4 percent towards either a Roth IRA, a college 529 plan, or both.

By contributing to a Roth, Orin can save for *both* retirement and college at the same time. "The Roth offers the invaluable benefit of liquidity. Most people don't even know that every dollar of Roth IRA contributions can be taken out at any time without penalty or taxes," says Maurer.

Only the gains that you have earned on your Roth are taxed when you withdraw money early, he adds—unless you are taking the money out *specifically* to pay for your child's education. So in Orin's case, this could be a pretty prudent way to have two expensive bases covered. (And remember, he can take out a loan for college if need be, but there is no such thing as a loan for retirement.)

Maurer also thinks that Orin may want to start making some small contributions to a 529 plan. This is a specific savings plan that provides some tax advantages when putting away money to fund your child's education. It's similar to an IRA in many ways, except it's for college savings, rather than retirement. You put after-tax dollars in a 529 and it is exempt from federal taxes when you withdraw to pay for college. It varies from state to state, but some actually allow you to deduct your contributions to a 529.

Orin needs to save gradually for his daughter's education, but he does not need to over compensate and save too much, too soon. "He has no idea how expensive or inexpensive his daughter's college may be. She could go to a state school, or she could get scholarships that will help reduce these costs," says Maurer. "There is no need to over-save, especially if it means spiting a comfortable lifestyle, retirement savings or the pursuit of a dream with a calculated price tag."

To Maurer, Orin should be plugging away at the Mayor's Lounge, especially because he has already borne the brunt of initial expenses by purchasing the property and doing the majority of the renovations. "Who knows, he could make three times as much from the Mayor's Lounge as he might need to pay for his daughter's education," says Maurer.

Orin is already deeply invested in the project and electing to give up—especially when he is so close to finishing—might cause him to take a loss.

Orin's cash flow situation will improve when his wife returns to work. But if she doesn't, Orin has also done such a solid job of contributing to his retirement (and buying a house) at a relatively young age that he could even elect to stop saving for a year if it will allow him to pursue one of his ventures, such as the Mayor's Lounge. "If he had very few 'one shot' years where he took that year's retirement savings to dump into a real estate or new business venture," Maurer says, "that may only serve to boost his eventual retirement savings if the projects are successful."

It's a risk, but he's already done enough early in life that he doesn't have to worry too much about playing catch up. He's already ahead of the game, by most standards. If he chooses to put some of this money into the Mayor's Lounge or any other real estate ventures, ultimately it's just another form of investing his money. It may be slightly risky, but some people will never be able to save or live in the box.

Orin is definitely one of those people.

And even though plans may change, people don't always have to.

13

The Roth 401(k)

THE FUTURE OF YOUR FUTURE?

First chocolate met peanut butter. Then Angelina Jolie met Brad Pitt. Then came the iPod cell phone.

Revolutionary pairings that change the way we live.

Now we may be looking at one new marriage that could change the way we retire: the Roth 401(k).

Don't discount the lack of sex appeal. This is a major development for us. We will be the first generation to grow up with this new retirement savings vehicle. It's yet another option that, if used properly, could allow us to enjoy more security in our retirements than any previous generation.

We don't need to bemoan the lack of a pension or Social Security benefits if we play by the new rules of retirement. We are being given more options to accumulate retirement savings—we just need to know what they are and take advantage of them.

The Roth 401(k) is one of the newest options that you will surely run into over the next several years. In short, it takes the tax advantages of the Roth IRA and applies it to the 401(k). Except you don't have to seek out these benefits independently, they're coming from your employers.

The water is being brought to the horse. Finally.

Employers were first officially allowed to offer Roth 401(k)s in 2006, so unfortunately they are not widespread just yet. But more and more employers have said that they will soon roll out Roth 401(k)s to workers over the next few years.[1]

This puts you in a position to make another move that could ultimately mean the difference in hundreds of thousands of dollars in retirement savings.

If your employer offers you both a Traditional 401(k) and a Roth 401(k), you will have to make an important top-line decision. From an investment standpoint, the Roth 401(k) functions just like the regular 401(k)—you choose from the same menu of funds your employer presents to you and you fund the account with ongoing contributions from your pay. That's about where the similarities end. In the next section, we find out how the Roth 401(k) works.

Roth 401(k) Features

Think about the difference between the Roth IRA and the Traditional IRA for a second. With a traditional IRA, you make contributions and you can deduct these contributions from your annual taxes. You lower your taxable income and get a short-term tax break. Your contributions and earnings also grow tax-deferred while you are working, but you will finally end up paying taxes once you start making withdrawals from the IRA during your retirement.

It's a save-now-and-pay-later savings concept.

With the Roth, you don't get any immediate tax breaks. You put money in straight from your net pay and you can't deduct a thing. Your contributions and earnings grow without being taxed—and when you retire the whole lot is yours. Every penny. It's a tax-free as opposed to tax-deferred savings account. You don't pay taxes on any income you withdraw from your Roth during your retirement.

It's a pay-now, have-more-later savings concept.

That is exactly the same concept that is at work with the Roth 401(k), just applied to a work-sponsored retirement plan rather than an individual one. Here are the highlights:

- When you make a contribution to a Roth 401(k), it comes out of your net pay. So you are using after-tax dollars to fund this account, as opposed to pretax dollars which go into a regular 401(k). Because you are using money that has already been taxed to fund a Roth 401(k), you don't have to pay any taxes on the backend when you withdraw for retirement. You have already paid the piper. At retirement, every cent in your Roth 401(k) belongs to you and only you.

- With your regular 401(k) you make contributions from your gross pay, which is your income that you have not been taxed on. You are lowering your annual taxable income with regular 401(k) contributions, but this means that you *will*, however, pay taxes when you withdraw from your regular 401(k) during retirement.
- Unlike the Roth IRA, you can contribute to a Roth 401(k) no matter how much money you earn. If your employer offers a Roth 401(k) you are eligible to participate. With the Roth IRA, if you earn more than $114,000 a year (or $166,000 as a couple), you are not eligible to contribute to a Roth IRA. With a Roth 401(k) there are no income limitations. This makes the benefits of a tax-free retirement savings vehicle even more accessible.
- You can contribute up to $15,500 a year to a Roth 401(k). While this is the same amount that you can contribute to a regular 401(k), it's also $11,000 more than you are currently permitted to contribute to a Roth IRA for a year. This significantly expands the amount of money you are now allowed to put away for tax-free savings. You can, if you are eligible, contribute the maximum levels to both a Roth 401(k) and a Roth IRA in the same year. (You cannot, however, put $15,500 in a Roth 401(k) and $15,500 in a regular 401(k). You can have both, but the total contributions cannot add up to more than $15,500 for a year).
- One more very important feature to note about the Roth 401(k). If your employer matches any contributions that you make to your Roth, your employer's contributions do not go into your Roth 401(k). They go into a traditional 401(k). With a Roth 401(k), if you get a match, you will have two separate 401(k)s: one consisting of your contributions and one comprised of your employer's contributions. You will be taxed when you make withdrawals from the traditional 401(k), which consists of your employer's matching contributions, for retirement. So remember, *your* contributions and earnings are tax-free with the Roth 401(k), not your employer's.
- When you retire, you can roll your Roth 401(k) over into a Roth IRA, which means you can leave your money in the account as long as you would like. With a traditional 401(k) or a traditional IRA, you *must* start taking your withdrawals when you turn 70.5 years old. It's a long way away, but it affords you some more freedom down the road.

You don't have to commit every idiosyncrasy to memory. Don't panic. If you're not eligible for a Roth 401(k) right now, and you're probably not, you will be at some point in the not-too-distant future. For now, just consider the basic concept of the Roth 401(k): you pay when you plant the seeds of your 401(k), but not at all when it comes time for the harvest.

If you ever get confused about any other levels of detail, don't worry. Table 13.1 provides a quick-and-dirty rundown of everything you need to know about the difference between the Roth 401(k), the Roth IRA and the Traditional 401(k).

Table 13.1   Comparison of Roth 401(k), Roth IRA, and Traditional 401(k) Retirement Plans

Roth 401k Plan	Roth IRA	Traditional 401k Plan
Employee contributions are made with *after-tax* dollars.	Same as Roth 401k plan.	Employee contributions are made with *before-tax* dollars.
Investment growth accumulates without any tax consequences.	Same as Roth 401k plan.	Investment growth is not subject to Federal and most State income taxes until funds are withdrawn.
No income limitation to participate.	Income limits: married couples, $160,000, singles, $110,000 adjusted gross income.	Same as Roth 401(k) plan. No income limitation to participate.
Contribution limited to $15,000 in 2006 ($20,000 for employees 50 or over).	Contribution limited to $4,000 in 2006 ($5,000 for employees 50 or over).	Same as Roth 401(k) plan.
Withdrawals of contributions and investment growth are *not* taxed provided recipient is at least age 59½ and the account is held for at least five years.	Same as Roth 401(k) plan.	Withdrawals of contributions and investment growth *are* subject to Federal and most State income taxes.
Distributions must begin no later than age 70½. (This may change.)	No requirement to start taking distributions.	Same as Roth 401k plan.

Source: Division of Compensation Data Analysis and Planning, Bureau of Labor Statistics, U.S. Department of Labor.

Which One Is Right for Me?

The good news is you have options.

The bad news is you have options.

When thinking about the Roth versus the regular 401(k), it all comes down to how and when you want to pay your income taxes.

If you are thinking "What's the difference if I pay taxes now or later?" it's a good question to be asking. You can't avoid taxes, but you can manage how much you pay.

You won't want to draw all of your retirement income off of traditional tax-deferred savings accounts like the regular 401(k) and the traditional IRA. You will just get hit too hard during your retirement when you will need the money the most.

Consider this: If you've amassed $1.5 million in traditional retirement vehicles and you're in the 33 percent tax bracket when you retire, you are going to give up roughly $500,000 of that total in taxes during your retirement.

"Just like it's important to diversify your investments, it's also critical to diversify your tax situation," says David Wray, executive director of the Profit Sharing/401(k) Council.

When you are making your decisions between a Roth 401(k) and a Traditional 401(k), you need to consider your current income level and tax rate.

The Roth may be the right move if you expect your current tax rate to be the same, or higher, when you are no longer working.

In theory, the younger you are, the more likely this is to be the case. You won't feel the immediate pinch from income taxes in the short term as much as you will when you are earning more money and you are in a higher tax bracket.

But let's just say that your tax bracket stays exactly the same during your retirement. Here's how the Roth 401(k) would work out to make more sense than the traditional:

Rob and Tom are twin brothers, 30 years old, who do everything together. They work together, make the exact same salaries, they're in the same 25 percent federal tax bracket and they plan to retire at the exact same age of 65.

They both will contribute $3,000 a year to their 401(k)s for the next 35 years until the retire.

Their money is invested exactly the same and they expect to get the same average investment returns of 8 percent on their 401(k)s before they retire.

Rob, however, has elected to use a Roth 401(k) and Tom uses a traditional.

Both brothers would have an account worth $577,294 when they turn 65.

Rob could withdraw every dollar in his Roth 401(k)—his retirement withdrawals will be tax-free.

Tom would only net $432,970 off of his traditional 401(k) because he will defer his taxes until he withdraws from his account.

To be fair, Tom will also be able to deduct a total of $31,500 from his taxes over the years for his traditional 401(k) contributions.

Rob will not be able to deduct anything.

Tom's tax savings during his working years of $31,500, however, are dwarfed by the $144,324 in tax payments he has to make at retirement off of his 401(k).

Even if Tom invests all of his tax savings wisely along the way to his retirement, it will be difficult for him to ultimately make up the difference in the end.

If he invested his $900 a year of deductible tax savings in the stock market and earned 8 percent returns on average, this could provide him with an additional income of $89,490 during his retirement— still not enough to make up for the $144,324 he had to pay in taxes on the withdrawal from his traditional 401(k).

Unfortunately, we have no way of knowing what kinds of tax rates we will deal with during our retirements. We can only deal with our current realities and make the best decisions based on the information we have at hand.

Consider the possibilities about your tax situation during retirement, but also think about how you could be spending your time during retirement as well. A lot of people now end up working part-time during their retirements, some for the money, some for health and medical benefits, and some just to stay fresh and motivated. Whatever the reason, it is still income that you will earn in addition to the retirement savings you may also be drawing an income from at the same time. Your income during your retirement may be higher than you think.

So do not think that when you retire you are just going to live off of your retirement income, you may want to leave your options open. The longer you work, the longer you preserve your retirement savings.

CHAPTER 14

Any Door Will Do

Day One.

Mark just landed a brand new job, his first shot at a real magazine in New York. It covers money and finance, two things he knows absolutely nothing about, but he doesn't care.

He's 22, close to desperate, and needs a foot in the door.

Any door will do.

This is a good-looking glossy magazine, he thinks sitting in on his first story meeting. It may even help pay some of his gradually accumulating expenses and bills.

The meeting's focus turns to Mark, and his editor, a crusty and very old school newspaperman, goes into detail about his first story assignment. It's on the leaders in syndicated lending. He'll need 1,200 words and he'll need it in three days—"Any questions, Mark?"

"What's syndicated lending?"

They share a laugh and his editor explains that it's simply a term used when a few banks team up to issue a large loan to one borrower in single portfolio. "Any more questions Mark?"

"What's a portfolio?"

No one laughs.

This wasn't one of his finer moments or one of his finer questions, but Mark has always been good at asking questions. He'd prefer to be good at other things such as throwing a 101 mile-per-hour fastball or playing the guitar as effortlessly as Wes Montgomery or Derek Trucks. But Mark's okay with his lot in life. It's not a glamorous skill he has honed, but it's a skill nonetheless.

At the age of 29, almost every penny he's earned has come from being inquisitive. Mark's still a reporter and has continued to make a living for almost the last eight years writing about other people's money. He's also in the process of authoring his first book, and of course it too is going to be about other people's money.

It's kind of funny the way the whole thing worked out, he thinks, because he never had an interest in finance and he certainly never took a course in economics when he was majoring in English in college.

He's also never been particularly good at managing his own money.

His first job out of college at a small newspaper paid him $320 a week, which added up to just a little under $17,000 a year. It wouldn't have been a bad salary—if he worked in the 1970s. But in 1999 it didn't give him a chance.

Journalism didn't pay very well, so he couldn't and didn't save. He didn't bother with a 401(k) because he figured he wouldn't be at the newspaper long enough to vest. Even though he didn't really know what vesting meant at the time.

A year later he started earning about $28,000 but he was also putting 60 percent of his take-home pay to his rent each month. He didn't bother with a 401(k) because he was living paycheck-to-paycheck, and he thought he had no money to spare. His credit card substituted for debit card because he rarely, if ever, had any money in his checking account.

Every day he would write about credit cards and the lifelong dangers of being in credit card debt. Then guiltily, after hours, he would submit his card—at restaurants and bars. On vacations, he couldn't resist, and he traveled a hell of a lot when he couldn't afford it.

Mark never bought anything of real material value and quite easily, in just a few years, he had $5,000 in real material credit card debt. All while his salary hadn't increased much either.

Then he started asking questions.

Where is my money going?

Why do I work the same hours as investment bankers and lawyers but earn in an entire year what they earn in a month? An off-month, no less.

Why don't I have anything—anything at all—to show for what I do?

Why don't I just go work at a ski lodge out West and be happy?

Isn't there a better way?

At first he thought it was all income-related, but the more asked, the more he learned that it's not always about assets. It can be just as much about your obligations or your liabilities.

It's not always about how much you earn, but how much you do with it.

Time was going to move on, one way or another, he thought. He needed to make time work for him, not against him.

He was a few months away from moving in with his girlfriend, who would become his wife. He had to do something. So he moved out of the brownstone he was renting along with three friends, an MTV *Real World*esque arrangement that he had no business living in to begin with.

He moved home. All of his former rent money went to credit cards. He wasn't completely debt-free when he moved out again in four months, but at least he wasn't embarrassed to tell his girlfriend about it anymore.

Time moved on. He got a new job, took a deep breath and put 3 percent of his new $50,000 salary into a 401(k) that matched his contributions dollar-for-dollar. He asked enough about his 401(k) to realize what a fool he would be if he didn't use it, especially now that he was *writing* about retirement plans like the 401(k) for a living.

He stopped paying off his credit card bills and started saving everything for a ring—$500 a month for two years. He asked everyone he knew what to do with his debt and he was told to transfer the credit card balance to cards that had 0 percent interest rates until he could start paying it off again.

More time moved on. He got married. He used some of the money he got as gifts on his wedding day to pay off the last of his credit card debt, the balance that wouldn't budge. He cut up his cards.

He got several raises and was able to pay the wedding money back to himself and his wife for the next few months, which he figured was better than paying the credit card companies. Finally, he'd be free.

For almost five years, he grew accustomed to paying credit card companies along with his rent and his utilities every month. It became just another utility bill. He learned to live without the money, so he asked around—now what?

He was told to start a Roth IRA because it would help him hedge his bets. He could save for retirement in the Roth, but if he needed the money in a few years to help buy his first home it wouldn't be a problem to get it out.

His credit card money became Roth money. He automatically had enough deducted from his bank account every month to contribute the max of $4,000 at the end of the year.

A little more time passed and he grabbed yet another job. He put his old 401(k) money into his Roth. He was making about $20,000 a year more at his new job, so he had some decisions to make. What's next?

Buy his first home? Have a baby? By his first home *and* have a baby?

How about another vacation first?

Mark got lucky, and he knows it. He backed his way into a job asking questions about money. If he hadn't, he might still be living paycheck-to-paycheck, or he'd be feeding the beast and just trying to tame his debt down a bit.

Maybe even worse, he might not have saved anything at all. He's saved close to $30,000 in the last few years, both in his Roth and a handful of money market accounts. He's hardly rich, but he knows he's far from poor. He doesn't think about retirement nearly as much as he thinks about his more immediate future, which he wouldn't be able think about at all if he hadn't saved some money over the last few years.

He can look forward without having to constantly look over his shoulder every month and pay for mistakes he made in his past.

The burden of debt is gone, but some of his spending ways still exist. They'll always exist. He's just not an "either-or" type guy.

He wants it all, even though he doesn't always know *exactly* the best way to get it.

He knows he doesn't have all the answers, far from it.

But he also knows that he can always ask the questions.

Prescription

I still have a lot of work to do. I may have tucked some money away in the bank, but it's not enough. My wife and I can't complain. We'll earn about $150,000 combined this year and we'll be able to keep saving in our Someday account at a pretty decent clip. I still shoot for $500 a month to go straight into savings, with another $333 going into my Roth IRA.

But now it's not just about savings at this point. Like it or not, I've grown up a bit. I'm not saving for someday anymore; someday is now.

I don't own a home, which is killing me. I've paid about $100,000 in total rent over the last eight years, and I have nothing to show for it. That's our next mission and it's not going to be easy.

I don't just need to figure out how much money we have saved and how much house we can afford. That's relatively simple math. I need to know how much house we *should* buy.

As a general rule, you should buy a home that's worth about two to two-and-a-half times your gross income, says Linda Leitz, a certified financial planner at Pinnacle Financial Concepts in Colorado Springs. Leitz suggests you try to keep it under two times your gross income whenever possible to make certain that you are not taking on a long-term commitment you might not be able to handle.

Also, she says that no more than 35 percent to 40 percent of your income every month should go towards paying your rent or mortgage.

I have never done a budget in my life, but if I want to buy a home, now I don't have a choice.

My wife and I need to collaborate on this too; we've been married for two years and we've really only functioned independently when it comes to saving.

We'll need to save about another $10,000 to $15,000 before we will have enough money for a down payment, which will probably cost us somewhere between $80,000 and $100,000 for an apartment of decent size.

(I love New York.)

We *will* save this together in a joint money market account, hopefully one that earns about 5 percent interest. No one will do this for us. I'll have to get this money automatically deducted from my paycheck, otherwise it will vanish. I think that's perhaps the most valuable lesson in personal finance I'll ever learn—come to terms with all of your tendencies and who you really are. If you don't trust yourself, police yourself. When it comes to money, I have to let logic stay ahead of my behavior. Thank you, direct deposit.

Over the next several months, I'll gradually move my own money that I have already saved into this new home account. I'll beg my wife to do the same. I'm tired of guessing what we have; I need to know.

Buying this house is too important. We both save for our retirements at a respectable rate, but that won't buy us freedom right now. We need to make our money work for us. We will always need a home, and from an investment standpoint, real estate is the only investment that really grows in line with inflation. I already know I don't want to bank my retirement on what our home-to-be might be worth in 35 years, and we've acted on that. I also know that I won't be able to adequately support myself during retirement if I don't ever own a home.

I don't aspire to be wealthy. I just want to be satisfied and secure.

I can't do it all at once, no matter how much I might like to. I can only just try to put the puzzle together one piece at a time.

CHAPTER

15

There Is a World of Help Out There

For better and for worse, we are the Google Generation. We have access to all of the information that we could ever want, yet often spend time Googling the names of friends, former friends, boyfriends, girlfriends, coworkers, and, of course, ourselves.

Everything you need to know about retirement, investing and saving is just a few clicks away. There is a ton of information out there and it can certainly be overwhelming at times, especially when you are looking for just one specific nugget.

I have tried to provide you with answers to any of the most fundamental questions that you have, but you will undoubtedly have other questions along the way. These are just a few sites that might help to fill in any blanks for you. Some will also offer articles and commentary on different methods for saving or various strategies for investing your retirement money.

Whether you are just getting going, or you have already set the wheels in motion, you should always be asking questions. The more you know, the more you can make decisions that will have direct impact on your financial security, both now and during your retirement.

There is a world of help out there. But it won't do us any good if we don't ask the questions. Here are a few places that you may want to look:

- *www.choosetosave.org*. This site is designed to encourage people to save and arm you with the financial education to do it properly.

The Employee Benefits Research Institute and the American Savings Education Council teamed up to put together a comprehensive site that offers you a number of free resources and suggestions that can help you to save more effectively. The site offers hundreds of different calculators that you can use, for example, to outline a thorough budget, figure out how much you should save for retirement, how to pay off your credit cards, or how to decide which IRA may be right for you. It also has a Ballpark E$timate worksheet that can give you a quick idea how much money you will need for a comfortable retirement. (You can do this all in Spanish too.) There are a number of brochures and savings tips on the site that are concise and easy to navigate. It doesn't overcomplicate investing or saving and does a good job of cutting to the chase.

- *www.morningstar.com.* If you have a question about investing, there is a good chance that the Morningstar site has the answer. Aside from providing reports on mutual funds, ETFs and stocks, just to name a few of the site's bread and butter functions, it also has a very helpful section on personal finance that runs through the ins and outs of basically every savings vehicle out there. This section is a great reference on 401(k)s, IRAs, 529 plans, and tax planning, and offers detailed articles and discussions on these topics in addition to basic explanations. There is also a Self-Study Workshop that can help you navigate through Investing 101 on your own and at your own pace, as well as a Personal Finance Forum that allows you to chat with other people on any subject you can think of.

- *www.401khelpcenter.com.* This site has three primary sections. The one for Plan Participants can tell you anything and everything you ever wanted to know about 401(k)s and other defined contribution plans. You can get anything from a basic outline of how a 401(k) plan works, to a calculator that will help you decide if you're better off in a Roth or a Traditional 401(k) plan. It can also give you some help on managing your 401(k) money properly, how to quickly give your 401(k) an annual check-up, and also offers a number of tips on topics such as how to balance debt with saving for retirement. If you are looking for any information on borrowing or withdrawing money early from your 401(k). The site can also serve as an excellent resource for guidance on both subjects.

- *www.mymoney.gov.* This is the federal government's website that is set up through its Financial Literacy and Education Commission. The section of Retirement Planning is robust; it essentially aggregates expertise from all of the federal government's agencies that focus on any retirement issues. For instance, it will guide you directly to the Department of Labor's research on retirement fees and expenses, or the IRS's guidelines on individual retirement accounts. (Publication 590). It also has booklets on how to begin saving for retirement and how to "take the mystery out of retirement saving." While it is a government site that contains a good deal of technical information, the resources featured are in very familiar terms and are generally user-friendly. This site is a great way to get from point A to point B and can quickly help you pull information from 20 government agencies. It also has a toll-free telephone number that you can call to get more information sent to you directly: 1.888.MYMONEY

- *http://finance.yahoo.com/personal-finance.* This is a relatively new feature to the Yahoo! Finance site that offers solid how-to guides, calculators, and expert analysis on retirement, saving, and budgeting, as well as real estate, insurance, taxes, and loans. The content is frequently updated, which can help you stay current with any new investment concepts or products as well as developments in the general retirement landscape. The how-to guides are great as well, particularly on subjects such as getting out of debt and saving, as well as maximizing the potential of your IRA. There is also a very thorough glossary that gives quick and easy-to-understand definitions for almost any financial term.

- *www.fairmark.com.* This site is a helpful guide to taxes for any kind of investor. While it doesn't specialize in retirement, it offers perhaps the most complete guide to Roth IRAs that you will find on the web, with over 100 pages of content dedicated to these accounts. It can get heavy into the minutiae, but it can also give you the basics right away. There is a "three-minute tour" of the Roth IRA on the site, as well as some simple rules of thumb and an outline of all the different ways that you could open up a Roth IRA. The site also offers a general guide to the Roth 401(k).

- *www.kiplinger.com.* One of the best sites around for news and resources on personal finance and retirement. The Your

Retirement section has a number of calculators and retirement tools that can help you determine how much you should be saving for retirement and project how much your 401(k) will grow over time. The site also houses some more general personal finance resources that can help you figure out things such as how much you can and should spend on housing, what it will take for you to become a millionaire, or even ways to calculate the real miles per gallon of your car. There are a number of columns on personal finance that can give you a good conversational feel for retirement and savings techniques, in addition to addressing some of the most critical components of saving your money efficiently.

- *www.bankrate.com.* This site offers a good deal of news and advice on a wide range of investment and savings subject. It can be one of the most useful tools on the Web for finding the best rates for money market accounts, mortgage rates, home equity loans, credit cards, or any other basic banking vehicles. If you are looking to open up either a checking or a savings account, for instance, the site will help you locate the best yielding on the market. You can search for the best rates in your specific state, or the site will also break down the best rates for any money market or checking accounts that you can open online as well. The site has other features, including information on college financing, which can help you find the best rates on national and local student loans.

- *www.401k.org.* This is the Profit Sharing/401(k) Council of America's site that is specifically dedicated to helping and educating participants in work-sponsored retirement plans. The site runs through all of the basics of 401(k) plans and provides a 401(k) calculator, retirement checkup, and a primer on taking out a loan from your retirement plan. There is a section on questions to ask if you are a looking for a good financial planner as well. The site also has several interactive 401(k) games—crossword puzzles, word searches, 401(k) matching games and an interactive 401(k) map—that are available in both English and Spanish. Seriously. Check the site too to find out when the next 401k Day is, it may be a good excuse to wear some casual clothing to "represent the leisure" you hope to enjoy during your retirement.

- *www.why401k.com.* As you could probably guess, this site offers a number of compelling reasons why you should be contributing to your 401(k). It also has a "(k)Check Calculator" which can help you figure out exactly how much you should be contributing to your 401(k). It will give you a number of different snapshot scenarios that will illustrate how various contribution levels will impact your net take home pay, while will also estimate what your 401(k) account balances could be when you retire based on these different contribution levels. Along with this snapshot, you can also get an idea just how much it would cost you in the long run if you waited a year to start participating.

CHAPTER 16

An Afterword

Trumpets and violins, I can hear in the distance.
I think they're callin' our name.
Maybe now you can't hear them,
but you will. . . .

—Jimi Hendrix, *Are You Experienced?*

I have read and listened to a number of interpretations of Hendrix's music and lyrics. And I am almost certain that he was not talking about retirement in these lines.

But it still rings true. Retirement is an inevitable reality for so many of us, yet so few actually even bother to consider it throughout the vast majority of our lives.

Why is it that at a young age we can envision what our future lives might look like in so many ways, yet retirement seems to rarely get a thought?

We can conjure up and articulate the images or the idealities of our future spouses without a single stutter. With ease we can indulge in fantasies about dream jobs, dream houses, and dream vacations and back again.

We clearly have no trouble considering the future; in fact, it may actually be one of the best methods to motivate through Today.

Our retirements, however, which could account for one-quarter of our lifetimes, seem to be the bastard stepchildren of Possibility.

It may be distant for us, but it is still real.

It is still a part of your life, even if it is not a part of your life right now.

We have time to support this reality with security. But that does not mean that we should wait. Small commitments now can translate into significant stability later, and the sooner this is put to work, the more truth this notion holds.

The longer we postpone planning and saving, the more we will have to make sacrifices today for the sake of tomorrow.

It doesn't have to be that way. You could make a simple decision to put yourself on autopilot right now. You could have 3 percent of your pay automatically deducted and contributed to a 401(k) today and it will have a major impact on the rest of your life. If you have already done that, then see if you can't find a way to increase this contribution a bit. Or put some money in an IRA if you want some more flexibility.

It will change your life if you let it.

It's not magic. It is just what will happen when you combine patience with diligence and awareness.

It's your money. You earned it. You can do whatever you like with it.

It's your life and it always will be, both now and later. But later is more closely related to now than you might think.

Hopefully.

Be good to yourself.

APPENDIX

Save Now or Die Trying

THE 10 COMMANDMENTS

1. Acknowledge That Your Retirement is a Reality, Even If It May Be 30 or 40 Years Away. Your retirement will cost you more money than you could possibly imagine and you don't want to wait and see if you can play catch-up. If you wait until your 40s to start saving for your retirement, you will never be able to recapture the power you had in your 20s and 30s. You will also have fewer expenses in your younger years, so no need to wait.

2. Don't Wait, Do Something Now. You are not entirely on your own, but it is up to you to take care of yourself. Commit to saving just a small portion of each paycheck for your retirement *before* you can spend it. If you're employer offers you a retirement plan at work, do this first. If not, there is no excuse. Open an IRA as soon as possible to start making a little money go a long way.

3. Whenever There is Free Money, Take It. If you are lucky enough to work for an employer who will make matching contributions to your retirement plan, *take their money*. Ideally, contribute enough to get the full match from your employer. Someone is giving you guaranteed money if you agree to save for your retirement. Only a fool would say no to this proposition.

4. Treat Your Retirement as Another Line Item Taken Out of Each Paycheck. Instead of making large annual contributions to your

155

retirement, have smaller contributions automatically deducted from your paycheck. And if you can't set it up to get automatically taken from your paycheck, ask your bank if you can set up a recurring payment to an IRA, or another type of savings account. It's easier to mentally commit—and say goodbye—to $83 from each paycheck, for example, instead of writing a check for $2,000 once each year.

5. If You Think You Can't Afford to Save, You are Probably Wrong. Contributions you make to a work-sponsored retirement plan, such as a 401(k) come from you gross pay. You use pretax money to save in these retirement plans, which means you are lowering your overall taxable income. Even saving as little as $90 a month will help you begin to accumulate some serious long-term wealth. Why? Because you have allowed yourself.

6. Take Advantage of the Power of Compounding.   The best investment decision you will ever make is to start saving money early. The younger you are, the more it can work for you. You will never be able to regain the compounding power that you now have in your youth. Put it away, leave it alone, and let it grow.

7. No Matter How Much Help You Think You Might Get When You Retire, Don't Count on It.   There are no sure things in life and retirement and your retirement is definitely *your* responsibility. It's totally unclear what the Social Security system will look like when we retire. But there is a good chance that it will provide us with a smaller portion of our retirement income than any other previous generation. Also don't even think about any money you might inherit one day. If it shows up, great. If not? You will never be able to make up for lost time. Make your own reality and forget possibility.

8. Understand the Difference Between Good and Bad Debt.   Credit card debt is bad debt; you get nothing in return but more debt if you don't pay it off expeditiously. It erodes your financial independence and your ability to save—for anything. Student loans or a mortgage loan, on the other hand, are considered good debt. They are both investments in yourself and your immediate future.

9. There Is No Such Thing as "The Point of No Return." It's never too late for you to learn how to make smarter moves with your money. There are no stupid questions, only stupid decisions. If you are ever unsure about anything related to your money and savings, no matter how simple your question may be, ask someone or simply look for the answer yourself. (It will be between you and Google.) Having a basic, fundamental understanding of how to save properly could mean the differences of thousands of dollars at the end of the day.

10. Don't Save for Tomorrow at the Expense of Today. Do everything in moderation. But don't stay home every night because you are too scared to spend. There is such a thing as oversaving if you never take the time to enjoy your youth. You don't need to save 20 percent to 30 percent of your income right now for your retirement. Making relatively small contributions to your retirement at an early age will give you a tremendous amount of flexibility throughout the rest of your life. The longer you wait, the more sacrifices you will likely have to make. Life doesn't always have to be an either/or proposition. Enjoy yourself.

B

Two Steps to a Budget

The only way you will ever be able to really know how much you could—and should—be saving is to actually outline your budget.

It sounds tedious, but you shouldn't guess how much you can spend versus save every month. You need to know. Fortunately, it doesn't have to be all that complicated.

Below is a worksheet put together with the help of James Kibler, president of Eldridge Financial Planning in New York. It only takes a couple of steps and a few minutes for you fill out and get a better idea of your real financial picture. You can even fill out most of the information off the top of your head, so no need to grab your checkbook or check your bank and credit card statements (although it couldn't hurt).

Pencil it in on the page or make photocopies for future use. A lot of financial planners and suggest that once you do your budget, post it on the fridge or someplace else where you will see it every day. It's a good reminder that will help you stay focused and motivated.

Step One: Your Minimum Savings

Fill in your monthly *gross* income: _____

Divide your gross pay by 10.

This is your *total* minimum savings: _____

Now subtract your monthly 401(k) contributions

This is your personal minimum savings level: _____

This is the easiest way for you to get an idea just how much money you should aim to save every month. This is money you will pay to yourself.

Just like your 401(k) contributions, consider your personal minimum savings level a fixed expense every month.

At first, use your personal minimum savings to build up an emergency fund that can cover at least three months of expenses in case you lose your job, or you have some sort of medical emergency that prevents you from working. Have your personal savings minimum directly deposited into a standard savings or money market account—something liquid that will allow you to easily access the money without paying early withdrawal penalties.

Once your emergency is fund established, then direct your personal savings amount into a Roth IRA.

Have part, or all, of your monthly savings directly deposited into a Roth IRA every month. Remember, you can only contribute $4,000 to a Roth every year, so that comes out to $333.33 a month.

If your personal minimum savings level is more than that each month, put the rest in a money market account or a savings account that gets you a decent interest rate. A lot of banks are offering more than 5 percent APRs if you set up savings accounts online these days. Just make sure there are no fees or minimum balances before you make your selection. You don't need to pay to save.

Step Two: Monthly Spending

Now that your savings is a fixed expense, you need to get a handle on just how much you should realistically be spending each month.

Fill in the worksheet on page 161 with all of your monthly expenses to figure out how much extra cash you may have after you pay yourself *and* your bills.

Do your best to live within this final box. It can help you get an idea for how much you should spend on food every week, which will likely be your largest expense here. Everything else is yours to do what you please; you worked for it. Save it for a vacation. Buy another iPod. Drink it away. I don't care. You earned it. Just live within your means.

You can't get where you want to go without some sort of road map and that is why this worksheet is here. It's not that difficult to get your bearings; and it's certainly easier than dealing with the consequences of spending blindly.

Don't guess what you should know.

And *always* remember to pay yourself.

Gross Monthly Income	
Divide by 10	
Minus 401(k) contribution	
Amount you should save	
Net Check (actual take-home pay each month)	
Minus Fixed Expenses	
Amount you should save	
Rent/Mortgage	
Electric/Gas	
Debt Payments	
Phone	
Cable/Internet	
Cell Phone	
Car Payments	
Insurance	
Other Fixed	
Total Fixed Expenses	
Left for food, dining out, and whatever it is you do when you do what you want to do	

APPENDIX C

Your Seven Rules of Thumb

There are more rules of thumb in personal finance than you have fingers and toes. Some are more helpful than others, but here are a few general rules you might want to keep in mind when it comes to saving or making important life purchases:

1. Save 10 to 15 percent of your gross pay, with a portion always dedicated to your retirement savings. If you wait until your 40s to start playing catch-up, this rule of thumb gets jacked up to 30 percent.
2. As soon as you start saving, put a portion of your savings towards an emergency fund that will cover three to six months of living expenses, in case you lose your job.
3. The easiest way to figure out how much to start saving for retirement? Never leave free money on the table. If you are eligible for a retirement plan at work and your employer will match your contributions up to a certain portion of your pay, always contribute enough to get the maximum match.
4. Never have more than 10 percent of your 401(k) money invested in your own company's stock (or any one stock, for that matter).
5. Housing expenses—rent/mortgage, maintenance and utilities— should account for 30 percent to 40 percent of your monthly gross pay. Anything more may seriously cripple your ability to save, or pay off existing debts. Also shoot to have about 25 percent going to food, clothing and fun. And never have more than 30 percent of your income going to debt and yes this includes mortgage payments.

6. Buying a home will help you gain financial independence—but do not buy too much house too soon. Advisors suggest that you buy a home that is 2 to 2.5 times your gross household income.

7. To get an idea of how much money you will need to retire, many financial advisors are now suggesting that people approaching retirement should have at least 10 to 15 times their current annual salary socked away. Figure that you will need 70 percent to 80 percent of your annual income to retire. You won't be retiring for a good 30 or maybe 40 years, but that should at least drive home how expensive it is to stop working.

About the Author

Mark Bruno, 29, is a reporter for Crain's *Pensions & Investments*, the largest and most credible publication in the retirement industry for the last 30 years. He has covered money management and retirement issues for *P&I*, and his stories have appeared in a number of other Crain's business publications. He has served as both a writer and editor for a wide range of investment and finance newspapers and magazines, including *FundFire* and *U.S. Banker*.

Self-taught in the world of finance and economics, Bruno wonders why authors always use the word "avid" to describe their passion for a hobby. He is also guilty, like many people in his age group, of thinking that life will always find a way to take care of itself. He laughed when his first employer used the word "retirement" and discussed the company's 401(k) plan. He knew nothing of finance, and even less about planning for something that was 40 years away when he had just barely finished living 21. He lost several years to save. Consequently, he also lost tens of thousands of dollars because of his ignorance.

Bruno is not sure at what point one officially becomes an expert in either finance or economics—but he knows he has already learned enough to understand that he and his generation cannot afford to wait any longer. More importantly, he can't wait to share what he's learned with his peers before it's too late.

An avid music-lover and runner, Bruno and his wife Wendy live in New York City.

Endnotes

Chapter 1

1. According to the Social Security Administration, the average monthly Social Security check is $958 per month.
2. Kaiser Family Foundation and the Health, Research and Educational Trust, *2005 Annual Survey of Employer Health Benefits*, http://www.kff.org/insurance/7315/upload/7315.pdf.
3. MSN Money, "Your retirement health-care bill: $200,000," http://articles.moneycentral.msn.com/Insurance/InsureYourHealth/YourRetirementHealthCareBill200000.aspx.
4. Statistics from a www.401k.org survey show that on matching contribution, 95 percent of 401(k) plans provide some form of company contribution. The most common type of company matching contribution is $.50 on the dollar, up to the first 6 percent contributed by the employee.
5. The Department of Labor's Employee Benefits Security Administration's *Private Pension Plan Bulletin* (2004 and 2006) reveals that active private-sector workers covered by a DB plan decreased from 30.1 million in 1980 to 21.6 million in 2002 (a decline of over 25 percent), while similar workers covered by a DC plan increased from 14.4 million in 1980 to 52.9 million in 2002.
6. Employee Benefit Research Institute, *Issue Brief* 299 (November 2006).

Chapter 2

1. The Retirement Group at Merrill Lynch, *Merrill Lynch Savings and Retirement Survey Targeting 18–30 Year-olds* (2005).

Chapter 3

1. Alicia H. Munnell, Francesca Golub-Sass, and Anthony Webb, *What Moves the National Retirement Risk Index? A Look Back and an Update*, Center for Retirement Research, Boston College, January 2007.
2. Social Security Administration, *The Annual Report of the Board of Trustees for the Federal Old Age and Survivors Insurance*, 1 May 2006, http://www.ssa.gov/OACT/TR/TR06/II_project.html.
3. Center for Disease Control and Prevention, U.S. Department of Health and Human Services, and the National Center for Health Statistics, *Health, United States, 2005*, http://www.cdc.gov/nchs/data/hus/hus05.pdf#027.

4. Michael Tanner, ed., *Social Security and its Discontents* (Washington, D.C.: The Cato Institute 2004).
5. Brightwork Partners on behalf of Putnam Investments, *Study of 5,400 working people over the age of 45,* January 2007.
6. U.S. Department of Commerce, *Report on Personal Savings,* January 2006.
7. U.S. Census Bureau, *Income, Poverty, and Health Insurance Coverage in the United States: 2005,* August 2006.

Chapter 5

1. U.S. Department of Labor, *Pension Protection Act,* http://www.dol.gov/ebsa/pdf/ppa2006.pdf.
2. Profit Sharing/401k Council of America, *49th Annual Survey of Profit Sharing and 401k Plans,* 6 October 2006.
3. Employee Benefit Research Institute, *Issue Brief,* Vol. 299 (November 2006).
4. 401khelpcenter.com, "401k Plan Loans—An Overview," http://www.401khelpcenter.com/loans.html.
5. Brenda Watson Newmann, *Don't Tap Your 401k to Pay Off Debt,* Morningstar Inc.
6. Income Tax Regulations Section 1.401(k)–1(d)(2).
7. U.S. Department of Labor, Bureau of Labor Statistics, *Number of Jobs Held, Labor Market Activity, and Earnings Growth Among the Youngest Baby Boomer:; Results From a Longitudinal Study* 25 August 2006, http://www.bls.gov/news.release/pdf/nlsoy.pdf.
8. Public Law 107-16, 115 Statute 38, Economic Growth and Tax Relief Reconciliation Act of 2001 (EGTRRA).

Chapter 7

1. Internal Revenue Service Publication 590, http://www.irs.gov/pub/irs-pdf/p590.pdf.

Chapter 9

1. Retirement Group at Merrill Lynch, *Merrill Lynch Savings and Retirement Survey Targeting 18–30 Year-Old,* 2005.
2. Prudential Retirement, *Fifth Annual Workplace Report on Retirement Planning,* 16 November 2006.
3. Takeshi Yamaguchi, Olivia S. Mitchell, Gary R. Mottola, and Stephen P. Utkus, "Winners and Losers: 401(k) Trading and Portfolio Performance," *Pension Research Council Working Paper No. 2006-26* (October 2006).
4. Retirement Security Project, Brookings Institute, *Automatic Investment: Improving 401(k) Portfolio Investment Choices,* 2005.
5. Vanguard Institutional, *How America Saves,* September 2006, https://institutional.vanguard.com/iip/pdf/CRR_HAS_2006.pdf.
6. Takeshi Yamaguchi, et al.

7. Julie Agnew, *Personalized Retirement Advice and Managed Accounts: Who Uses Them and How Does Advice Affect Behavior in 401(k) Plans?* Center for Retirement Research at Boston College, March 2006.
8. Hewitt Associates, *Trends and Experiences in 401(k) Plans*, 2005.
9. Hewitt Associates, *401k Evolution—Coming Full Circle—Part Two: Managed Accounts*, 2005.

Chapter 11

1. The Experian Poll, November 2006, cited in Mindy Fettermen and Barbara Hansen "Young people struggle to deal with kiss of debt," *USA Today,* 22 November 2006.
2. Nellie Mae cited in Paige Ingram, "Credit card debt a challenge for college-age students," *Evansville Courier Press*, 5 July 2006.
3. U.S. Department of Education, National Center for Education Statistics, *National Postsecondary Student Aid Study* for 2003–2004, 1999–2000, 1995–1996, and 1992–1993.
4. Index Credit Cards, Credit Card Monitor, http://www.indexcreditcards.com/creditcardmonitor., 25 January 2007.
5. Bradley Dakake, *Deflate Your Rate: How to Lower Your Credit Card APR*, U.S. PIRG Education Fund, Boston, 27 March 2002.

Chapter 13

1. Fairmark Press, "Roth 401k Overview," *Tax Guide for Investors*, http://www.fairmark.com/rothira/roth401k/overview.htm. *Note:* Based on a Fairmark study in which the early survey responses indicated about a third of employers that have 401(k) plans planned on adding this feature as of January 1, 2006. The actual number, however, may have been smaller.

Index